THE
HBCU
EXPERIENCE

THE GRAMBLING STATE UNIVERSITY EDITION

Visionary Author: Dr. Ashley Little
Lead Author: Ahvery N. Thomas, Esq.
Foreword Author: Dr. Edwin B. Thomas, Sr.
Foreword Author: Dr. David "Rusty" Ponton

Published By: The HBCU Experience Movement, LLC

The HBCU Experience Movement, LLC

thehbcuexperiencemovement@gmail.com

Ordering Information:
Quantity Sales: Special discounts are available on quantity purchases by corporations, associations, and nonprofits. For details, contact the publisher at the address above.

Photo Credit: Ahaski N. Thomas, MAT
Edwin B. Thomas, Jr.
Zhari G. Thomas
Gerard Howard

ISBN: 979-8-218-20275-0

DR. ASHLEY LITTLE

A Message from the Founder
Dr. Ashley Little

Historically Black Colleges & Universities (HBCUs) were established to serve the educational needs of black Americans. During the time of their establishment, and many years afterward, blacks were generally denied admission to traditionally white institutions. Prior to The Civil War, there was no structured higher education system for black students. Public policy, and certain statutory provisions, prohibited the education of blacks in various parts of the nation. Today, HBCUs represent a vital component of American higher education.

The HBCU Experience Movement, LLC is a collection of stories from prominent alumni throughout the world, who share how their HBCU experience molded them into the people they are today. We are also investing financially into HBCUs throughout the country. Our goal is to create a global movement of prominent HBCU alumni throughout the nation to continue to share their stories each year, allowing us to give back to prestigious HBCUs annually.

We are proud to present to you *The HBCU Experience: The Grambling State University Edition.* We would like to acknowledge and give a special thanks to our amazing lead author / partner, Ahvery N. Thomas, Esq., for your dedication and commitment. We appreciate you and thank you for your hard work and dedication on behalf of this project. We would also like to give a special thanks to our foreword authors, expert authors, contributing authors and partners for believing in this movement and investing your time, and monetary donations, to give back to your school. We appreciate all of the Notable Grambling State University alumni who shared your HBCU experience in this publication.

About Dr. Ashley Little

Dr. Ashley Little is Ms. Georgia Global Continental 2023 and the CEO/Founder of Ashley Little Enterprises, LLC, which encompasses her media, consulting work, writing, ghost writing, book publishing, book coaching, project management, magazine, public relations & marketing, and empowerment speaking. In addition, she is an award-winning serial entrepreneur, TV/radio host, TEDx speaker, international speaker, keynote speaker, media maven, journalist, writer, host, philanthropist, business coach, investor, advisor for She Wins Society, and 21-times award-winning bestselling author. As seen on Black Enterprise (2X), *Forbes* (2X), *Sheen Magazine* (Print and Online), Sheen Talk, Voyage ATL, Fox Soul TV, NBC, Fox, CBS, BlackNews.Com, Shoutout Miami, Shoutout Atlanta, Morning Star, Yahoo Finance, Heart and Soul, The Book of Sean, *HBCU Times, VIP Global Magazine*, The Black Report, Vocal, Ted.com, Medium, Soul Wealth, Hustle and Soul, BlackBusiness.com, Glambitious Top 21 Women Of 2021, New York Weekly's Top 10 Hardest Working CEOs alongside billionaire Mark Cuban, *US Insider's* Top 10 Women Entrepreneurs alongside billionaire and media mogul, Oprah Winfrey, *London Daily Post, Sheen Magazine* 5 Pioneers Making a Difference in Their Communities, NCA&T *Alumni Times*, CEO Weekly Top 10 Influential People in 2021 alongside billionaires Jeff Bezos and Beyonce' and many more. Through the Biden & Harris Administration, and Leaders Esteem Christian Bible University, she was also awarded with the Presidential Lifetime Achievement Award the highest award in the country. She is the Chancellor for Leaders Esteem Christian Bible University(Atlanta campus), and board member as well. Charter member for Dr. Judy Rashid Leadership and Education Center in South Africa.

As a recipient of the "Author of The Year" award by Glambitious, she is also a part of The Forbes Next 1000 Class of 2021 in partnership with Square. This first-of-its-kind initiative celebrates bold and inspiring entrepreneurs who are redefining what it means to run a business. Furthermore, she was a recipient of Nashville's Black 40 Under 40 Awards in December 2021. It is an annual event honoring the best and the brightest for their accomplishments in their chosen field and for their contributions and commitment to the African American community. Dr. Little is also an official member of For(bes) The Culture. For(bes) The Culture was formed in Boston at the Forbes Under 30 Summit in October of 2017. They pride themselves on convening current and future black and brown leaders worldwide to network, collaborate, share opportunities, and discuss issues related to their communities and the planet at-large. She was recognized along with other influential leaders and distinguished entrepreneurs, including Oprah Winfrey, Mel Robbins, Gary V and many more for the annual Brainz 500 Global Awards List awarded by *Brainz Magazine*. Lastly, she is a proud member of The Chancellor's Round Table at North Carolina A&T State University and 2022 Recipient of the Dr. Velma Speight Young Alumna Award at North Carolina A&T State University.

She is a proud member of Delta Sigma Theta Sorority, Incorporated, and a member of Alpha Phi Omega. She is very involved in her community, organizations and non-profits. Currently, she is the co-founder of Sweetheart Scholars non-profit organization, along with three other powerful women. This scholarship is given out annually to African American females from her hometown of Wadesboro, North Carolina who are attending college to help with their expenses. Dr. Little believes it takes a village to raise a child and she also encourages others to never forget where you come from. Dr. Little is a strong believer in giving back to her community. She believes our young ladies need vision, direction and strong mentorship. She is the CEO/Founder/Visionary Author of The HBCU Experience Movement, LLC, the first Black-owned company to launch books written and published by prominent alumni throughout the world who attended Historically Black Colleges & Universities (HBCUs). As authors, they share a powerful collection of stories on how their unique college experience has molded them into the people they are today. The purpose of The HBCU Experience Movement is to change the narrative by sharing Black stories and investing financially back into our HBCUs to increase young alumni giving and enrollment. The award-winning bestselling authors won the Black Authors Matter TV Award in May of 2021, Inaugural Anthem Awards of 2022, as well as the International Book Awards by The American Book Fest. The books are also part of the WorldCat.org, the world's largest network of library content and services. Dr. Little is also the Editor and Chief of *Creating Your Seat at The Table International Magazine*, advisor for She Wins Society, and writing and publishing coach for the WILDE Winner's Circle.

She is the founder and owner of T.A.L.K. Radio & TV Network, LLC, which airs in over 167 countries, and streams live on Facebook, YouTube, Twitter and Periscope. This broadcasting and media production company is for new or existing radio shows, television shows, or other electronic media outlets to air content from a centralized source. All news, information or music shared on this platform are solely the responsibility of the station/radio owner. She is also the owner and creator of Creative Broadcasting Radio Station, the station of "unlimited possibilities." She is also one of the hosts of the new TV Show *Daytime Drama* nationally syndicated television show, which will be aired on Comcast Channel 19 and AT&T Channel 99 in 19 middle Tennessee counties. It will also air on The United Broadcasting Network, The Damascus Roads Broadcasting Network, and Roku.

Dr. Little is a 21X award-winning bestselling author of, *Dear Fear, Volume 2: 18 Powerful Lessons of Living Your Best Life Outside of Fear; The Gyrlfriend Code, Volume 1; I Survived; Girl, Get Up and Win; Glambitious Guide to Being an Entrepreneur; The*

Price of Greatness; The Making of a Successful Business Woman; and *Hello, Queen.* She is a co-host for The Tamie Collins Markee Radio Show, award-winning entrepreneur who is also a reflection contributor for the book, NC Girls Living in a Maryland World, Sales/Marketing/Contributing Writer/Event Correspondent for *SwagHer Magazine,* contributing writer for MizCEO Magazine, contributing editor for *SheIs Magazine,* contributing writer/national sales executive for *Courageous Woman Magazine,* contributing writer for Upwords International Magazine (India), and contributing writer/global partner for Powerhouse Global International Magazine (London). Host of "Creating Your Seat At The Table", Host of "Authors On The Rise", Co-Host Glambitious Podcast, Partner/Visionary Author of The Gyrlfriend Code The Sorority Edition along with The Gyrlfriend Collective, LLC. Lastly, she has received awards, such as "Author of the Month"; The Executive Citation of Anne Arundel County, Maryland Award, which was awarded by the County Executive Steuart L. Pittman; and Top 28 Influential Business Pioneers for *K.I.S.H. Magazine* Spring 2019 Edition. She has been featured in *All About Inspire Magazine, Formidable Magazine, BRAG Magazine,* the front cover of MizCEO Magazine in November of 2019, the front cover for Upwords Magazine in the October 2019 Edition, *Courageous Woman* Special Speakers Edition in November 2019 and *Influence Magazine.* She has been featured on a nationally syndicated television show, *HBCU 101,* on Aspire TV, Dynasty of Dreamers *K.I.S.H. Magazine* Spring 2019 Edition, the front cover of *Courageous Magazine* in December of 2019, the front cover of Doz International Magazine in January 2020, Top 28 Influential Business Pioneers for K.I.S.H. Magazine, *Power20 Magazine Glambitious* January 2020 and *Power20 Magazine Glambitious* February 2020. She was also featured in *Powerhouse Global International London Magazine* March 2020 edition, *National Boss Magazine* in the October 2020 edition, *Sheen Magazine* February 2020 edition as one of "The Top 20 Women to Be on The Lookout for in 2020", BlackNews.com, BlackBusiness.com, the front cover of *She Speaks Magazine* August

2020 edition, as well as the front cover of *National Boss Magazine* November 2020 edition.

In addition, she's been featured on BlackNewsScoop.com, awarded the National Women's Empowerment Ministry "Young, Gifted & Black Award" in February 2020, which honors and celebrates women in business below age 40 for their creativity and business development. Featured in *National Women Empowerment Magazine, Black Enterprise*, as well as on Fox, NBC, and CBS, she was interviewed on *The Black Report* on Fox Soul TV and the front cover for *National Boss Magazine*. She was also a speaker at The Black College Expo 2020, for Creative CEOs Summit in January of 2021, and international speaker for Living Your Dream Life Summit 2021. She was also the speaker for the Elite Business Women Powershift Conference 2021, The Bella, The Brand & Her Bag Wealth Summit 2021, The Unstoppable You Summit in January 2021, the Marketing Mastery Summit for Glambitious 2021, the Crown Yourself Conference in January 2021, as well as the Door Dash Virtual Black History Month Celebration. As the speaker for Day of Aggie Generations with North Carolina A&T State University, Dr. Little was the 2021 Woman of Black Excellence Honoree, guest speaker on the podcast, The Happy Hour Show, speaker for the Phoenix Jack & Jill HBCU Author Showcase, as well as a guest on The JMosley Show. As contributing author for *Prayers for The Entrepreneurial Woman* book, she has spoken at Creative Con, been recognized as one of Today's Black History Makers, as well as being a featured speaker at From Paper to Profits Conference. She has been afforded the opportunity to gain press access for "Don't Waste Your Petty" movie as well as Mahalia Jackson's movie. She's been a speaker for HerStory Women's Global Empowerment Summit, HerStory Women Who Lead Conference, Stepping N2 Sisterhood Sharing Winning Secrets Virtual Summit, I AM Glambitious Virtual Conference, Black Authors Matter TV show, Thought Leaders Global Virtual Summit, as well as A Conversation with Floyd Marshall, Jr. As a Black Authors Matter TV award winner, Grind Pretty Magazine, Revolt. She has spoken for Sheen Talk and served as the foreword author for the anthology *It Cost to Be the Boss*. Recognized by *VIP Global Magazine* as one of the Top 50 Most Influential Women, she has spoken at Black Writers Weekend, The GameChangers with Angela Ward Show, and served as keynote speaker for Blacks in Nonprofits Conference. Having served as speaker for the Leap Conference, Pass the Mic Sis, the From Purpose to Profit Summit, and The Been Worthy Podcast, she has been the speaker and host for The MizCEO graduation, was featured in *Emoir Magazine* for Building a Global Media Empire, Front Cover GlamCEO Magazine December 2022 and was a Making Black History Today recipient for Glambitious, 2023 Woman To Watch for Glambitious, 20 Black Women Entrepreneurs To Watch for BlkWomenHustle, Guest/Speaker on Glambitious Inaugural Live Talk Show Series, Model for Black Beauty Expo 2023, Recipient of The Champion Of Change Award from Colour Me Social Foundation, Black Women Making History for BlkWomenHustle, Speaker/Honoree at The Stepping N2 Sisterhood Conference 2023.

Dr. Little received her undergraduate degree in English from North Carolina A&T State University. She received her master's degree in Leadership and Coaching and her Doctorate in Leadership, as well. Dr. Little is a mover and shaker, and she continuously pushes herself to be better than she was yesterday. She gives God all the credit for everything that has happened in her life. She has strong faith and determination to be great. She believes her only competition is herself. Her favorite scripture is Philippians 4:13: "I can do all things through Christ who strengthens me."

Table of Contents

continued...

DR. EDWIN B. THOMAS, SR.

Foreword
Dr. Edwin B. Thomas, Sr.

As in the Black Panther movie, Historically Black Colleges and Universities (HBCUs) are like a modern day Wakanda Forever for those who have had the opportunity to attend one. HBCUs give students a cultural experience like no other. They were created during the mid- to late-1800's to provide higher education opportunities to African Americans who were not allowed to attend Predominantly White Institutions (PWIs) at a time of the post emancipation proclamation period. Over the years, HBCUs have grown culturally significant to those students who need a nurturing environment of learning at the higher educational level.

African American students acquire a family type atmosphere at HBCUs that allows them to feel at home. Unlike some other institutions, students are not just a number, professors treat them as individuals. The faculty often takes a personal interest in their students, therefore, some professors will do whatever they can to make sure students have what they need to do well academically. The saying "it takes a village to raise a child" is an old African proverb and it also encompasses how students are valued at HBCU institutions. Those instructors really take an interest in their students. If a person wants to learn, they will get the attention they need to obtain a great education. You see, a person can enroll at such an institution with low scores from a standardized test. These tests were designed to predict the success of a student in higher education. It is HBCUs that have made this a false assumption. These institutions take students where they are when they enroll and closes that educational gap to allow these students to succeed and graduate with college degrees. The value of an education from an HBCU has been questioned in the past. But that is a belief that has been proven to be just the opposite. In fact, graduates of HBCUs who later attend Predominantly White Institutions (PWIs) have enrolled into graduate programs and done outstandingly well. These include professional degrees that have produced outstanding doctors, lawyers, and engineers. Had it not been for these individuals starting their education at an HBCU, they may never have had the chance to become the professionals they are today. Not many years ago, the statement was made, "Are HBCUs still relevant?" The answer to that statement is a definite YES. For without the existence of these institutions many African Americans would not have had the opportunity to acquire a college education.

I believe this culture of teaching African American students with the passion for them to succeed came from the period of segregated schools. The teachers who taught at the so-called "colored" elementary through high school levels during that period were educated at an HBCU. These educators were dedicated to making sure that their students learned no matter what it took. They would not continue to a new lesson until the students understood it well enough to move to the next. Unlike today, teachers follow a curriculum plan that is set to move from lesson to lesson whether or not a student has comprehended it or not. From my experience during that time, those teachers took a personal interest in educating me, the same as the educational culture is at HBCUs. As mentioned earlier, the African proverb "it takes a village to raise a child" was present during the early days of my education. The teachers I had at that time knew my mother because some of them sang together with her in the church choir and others were a part of the same social organization. So, when I missed a homework assignment or failed a test, she found out. I could not get away with anything when it came to education. Therefore, I got tired of being on the receiving end of some type of punishment. As a result, I started doing my best in school and I scored well on the annual standardized test we took every year. This was true not only for me, but also for my brothers and sisters. Because of those dedicated caring teachers and my mother, we all successfully received college educations. Although I was satisfied obtaining a bachelor's degree, I was encouraged to continue my education to enroll into graduate school at a PWI, in which I didn't have the confidence at the time. As my teachers invested time in me to learn, my college professors invested time in me to be prepared beyond what I thought I was ready for educationally. I was the first person in my family to receive an advanced degree. From that experience, I noticed the difference between an HBCU and a PWI. All the graduate faculty for my program were white. Only one of the professors during my graduate school experience for my master's degree showed a personal interest in my success. This was totally different from my tenure during my undergraduate years. However, my HBCU professors had faith in me successfully completing my graduate degree at the PWI. I later furthered my education with a doctoral degree which was possible with the foundational education from an HBCU. I now follow the example of my HBCU professors. I take a personal interest in my students because I want to see them succeed in their careers as well as life.

Over the past 50 years, most African American families had first generation members graduating college. Even today, there are HBCU graduates who are the first generation in their family to graduate from college. Many of the members of these families would not have had this opportunity without the existence of HBCU institutions. Over time, these institutions played a significant role in providing higher education to African Americans for over a century. Traditionally HBCUs give a different experience of college life to their students. There is, definitely, a cultural difference in college life that sometimes is adopted by PWIs. One such difference happens during football season between halftime performances. While halftime is usually a time for fans to go to the concession stands, at an HBCU game it's a time of an anticipated performance by the school's marching bands in which no one leaves their seats until afterwards. In addition, there's the tradition of the social fraternities and sororities who step, stomp, and stroll around campus during special events while supporting and bringing attention to important African American issues around the nation. Without HBCUs, African Americans in the United States would not have progressed as it has done over the years.

HBCUs over the time of their existence have been a celebration of African American culture. Although they only exist on the east coast with a portion of the midwest to the southern regional states, they are well known around the country and in some cases, the world. These institutions embraced a rich history of an educational era that was created for a group of citizens at a time of racially motivated unrest. They have produced such alumni as Martin Luther King, Jr. and others who have made significant contributions to society, the nation, and the world.

About Dr. Edwin B. Thomas, Sr.

The New Iberia, Louisiana native, Dr. Edwin Thomas, appointee of the Clayton A. Wiley and the Viola E. Wiley Endowed Professorship in Engineering Technology at Grambling State University is person of many talents. He is an Associate Professor and Interim Department Head for the Department of Engineering Technology and also an Associate Band Director for the World Famed Tiger Marching Band. To the students who know him, he is a person who cares and shows concern about their academic well-being. One would have to talk to his many students, pass and present, to understand why. He has always been an inspiration to all that have had the pleasure of being one of his students. He is a graduate of Grambling State University where he received his BS degree in the field of Industrial and Engineering Technology. He received his MS degree from Northwestern State University in Engineering Technology and has earned two Doctoral degrees in education and music from Grambling State University and the American Conservatory of Music respectively.

Dr. Thomas' leadership role includes serving as a Program Coordinator for the Drafting and Design Engineering Technology concentration area within the department he chairs at Grambling State University. He has been a team member and leader for four ABET (Accreditation Board for Engineering and Technology) accreditation visits where he was responsible for developing and defending the self-study components for different programs and concentrations.

Dr. Thomas has a broad but solid background in engineering technology which includes professional work experiences in mechanical, structural, electrical, and architectural design assignments. He has work with several Architects, Engineers and

Contractors from around the state on several campus and community projects, including the Eddie Robinson Museum and the Conrad Hutchinson, Jr. Performing Arts Center at the university. In addition, Dr. Thomas was selected as a consultant and lecturer for the Louisiana State Department of Economic Development, Division of Economically Disadvantaged Business Development, Louisiana Contractor's Accreditation Institute. He was among a group of university professors from around the state who was chosen to help minority contractors become qualified for small business bond assistance. His services to these minority businessmen and women took him around the State of Louisiana where his instruction became popular to many around the state. In addition, he also served as a professor for a collaborative distant learning degree program in Project Management for the University of Louisiana System. The program allowed non-traditional working students to complete a Bachelors of Science degree by enrolling into one of the nine institutions within the system through online coursework.

Dr. Thomas' research interest includes academic support for African American students majoring in engineering technology programs and automated applications of engineering/technology related software to simulate problem solving. He has several technical certifications related to computer-aided drafting and design and computer system administration. He was selected by one of our sister institutions to work with a team of faculty members on a grant proposal to implement computer simulations related as a part of a study into the engineering technology curriculum at Grambling State University. It included the development of simulation modules on improving the understanding of fundamental engineering principles as it related to engineering technology. A team he was a part of was recently awarded a grant that will allow improved broadband access on campus as well as expand training to faculty and students in key areas such as telehealth, telemedicine, cybersecurity, Cisco IT areas, and online teaching among other research and grant collaborations.

His publications include a study of the Computer-Aided Design training for a major company titled "An Evaluative Study of Mechanical CAD Training" and a research study titled "The Impact of Cognitive and Non-Cognitive Factors on the Performance of African American Engineering Students in Mathematics." Other creative efforts include the design and consulting of many designs of buildings and structures in and around the community in which he sometimes includes his students. These projects have given students the opportunity to experience first-hand some of the responsibilities they will encounter during a career in an area of their chosen field.

On his musical side, Dr. Thomas has performed and recorded with various musical artists and celebrities. He has also consulted and collaborated with network producers interested in developing television appearances of the band. Working with the university's music faculty and staff, he created the conceptual design of the Conrad Hutchinson, Jr. Performing Arts Center, current home of the World Famed Tiger Marching Band.

Dr. Thomas was also a member of the World Famed Tiger Marching Band where he served in many student leadership roles and had the privilege of being the Head Drum Major. He was later asked by Professor Conrad Hutchinson himself to join his band staff, a most significant honor. He elevated through different levels of director positions including having the opportunity to lead the unit as Interim Director of Bands during the 2018-2019 academic year.

Dr. Thomas' involvement with the band over the years has been invaluable. His unique ability to visualize artistic field show designs has elevated him to developing several precision drills for the band while collaborating with fellow band staff members. He has worked as the concert band's co-director and directed the Pep and Traveling Marching Bands. He has also coordinated the selection, training, and supervision of all student leaders. Another major responsibility and accomplishment is that he manages and directs Grambling's

"Drumline," a marching percussion group that operates and performs on numerous occasions as an independent extension of the marching band. Its popularity and highly-demanded performances have led to additional donations and honorariums to the band program. He is the former advisor for the Kappa Kappa Psi Band Fraternity and has serve as an advisor of the Tau Beta Sigma Band organization in the past 40 plus years. In addition, he has served as a liaison between the current band and the band alumni in which he's always had a great relationship.

Dr. Thomas' mission is to increase the retention of the freshmen and upperclassmen students in both the Department of Engineering Technology and band. His focus is to pilot a program that will service the academic success of the new and current students. The goal is to develop an academic support program for students majoring in engineering technology. He prides himself as a person who interacts well with the students along with colleagues and works to serve as a positive role model. He is a part of several departmental, college, and university committees. He is a member of the American Society for Engineering Education (ASEE) and several other professional, honorary, and social organizations.

He is a husband, father, and grandfather to wife Rhonda, children Ahsaki, Ahvery, and Edwin, II and grand-daughter Zharia.

DR. DAVID "RUSTY" PONTON

Foreword
Dr. David "Rusty" Ponton

Growing up in a household of African American educators/HBCU graduates, during the end of segregation, the start of integration had its definite advantages and disadvantages. The advantages included continued high expectations for academic excellence, unwavering support for post-secondary education and constant reminders that an education was the best way for African Americans to battle the racial, social and economic injustices that we as African Americans faced in America. The disadvantages included self-induced pressure to over achieve, anxieties due to fear of failure and constant scrutiny by peers and teachers to outperform and surprisingly many times to even underperform. I went from being applauded for making all A's to "He thinks he's better than us" by my peers who looked like me and those who didn't accused me of trying to be white like them. It was a constant struggle to balance academic excellence with acceptance by those who looked like me and those who didn't.

My first interaction with teachers outside my home was at the segregated black school, Phyllis Wheatley which serviced grades one through twelve for African American students from my hometown and Melville, Louisiana and surrounding smaller towns. The teachers, staff and administrators were all products of Historically Black Colleges and Universities. The two primary institutions of higher learning represented were Southern University Agriculture & Mechanical and Grambling State University. Both of these HBCUs were nationally known for producing leaders and trendsetters in the fields of education, agriculture, science, technology, engineering and math (STEM). These alums prided themselves on being the best, academically, athletically and socially. It was no question that the biggest rivalry in all of HBCUs was between these two storied institutions. The pride and professionalism that was taken in preparing us daily by our teachers, staff members and administrators was unequaled. They were intentional in their actions on producing well-prepared, talented, socially conscious hard-working citizens poised to make a difference in the world. Then there was the 1954 U. S. Supreme Court landmark ruling in Brown vs. Board of Education of Topeka, Kansas which unanimously found racially segregated schools to be unconstitutional and in violation of the 14th Amendment and federally banned segregated schools!

Desegregation or integration as we knew it, would become the defining educational policy of the century. Many African American educational historians may argue that for all its intended good desegregation initially hurt the very people it was meant to help. As an elementary student coming up in a newly integrated school system, I had to work twice as hard as the white students that I shared classes with. I remember being conscious of the fact that now most of my teachers didn't look like me. They didn't motivate me, hold me accountable or inspire me to be my best. They were more concerned on how to integrate the class than teach me. I did have some white teachers who recognized that I was advanced beyond my years academically. They also saw in me the ability to further my educational goals. I keenly remember that as a fourth grader, I tested high school levels on the national standardized tests in reading, math and science. My fourth grade teacher recognized that fact and reinforced my abilities by giving me work outside the prescribed curriculum that was more challenging. She would also give me additional duties as a peer tutor for my classmates who needed help with subjects that they struggled with. There was a white classmate who struggled with reading and my teacher felt that I could peer tutor him thirty minutes a day when everyone else would be working on class assignments. He was excited to receive additional help and I enjoyed helping. We became close friends and he showed remarkable increases in his vocabulary and reading skills. When the teacher was asked by his parents what was the catalyst for his increased reading skills success, she informed his parents that I had been tutoring him thirty minutes a day one on one during class. His parents became highly upset and told the teacher explicitly to STOP! They did not want their son tutored by a black boy.

It was during my middle school and high school days that I reestablished the connections with HBCU teachers and the importance of an HBCU education. These insightful and progressive teachers challenged us to be our best and to critically think and question the norms. They made us look at higher education as the best pathway to success. Yes it would be hard, however the gains far outweighed the toil and labor that it took to make it. They also made us strongly consider our choices of where we would continue our postsecondary education. Although both my parents were Southern University graduates, I had strong ties to Grambling State University as well. I was fortunate in that I had athletic as well as academic options to continue my educational pursuits. I was offered an athletic scholarship to then perennial SWAC men basketball champions Alcorn State University under legendary coach Davey Whitney and also to Grambling State University under hall of fame coach Fred Hobdy. There were also athletic offers from predominantly white institutions (PWI's) and junior colleges. Ironically due to my ACT scores and GPA, I was afforded more academic offers than athletic offers. Louisiana State University, United States Military Academy, Northwestern University and Southern University A & M Baton Rouge were among the many choices I had on the table. Although I desperately wanted to continue my athletic career in college, I knew academics would be the priority and a HBCU would be my choice where I would want to continue my education. I chose Southern University A & M School of Engineering.

I completed my mechanical engineering technology degree in four years and graduated the top graduate in the school of engineering, 1986 with cum laude honors while also achieving my dreams of playing collegiate basketball. I went on to become the first black engineer at Owen's Corning Fiberglas, Kansas City, Kansas plant where I was a quality control process engineer. After a short stint with Owen's Corning, I took a position with Shell Oil Company as a retail marketer. I was the only African American in the district. When I questioned my District Manager about furthering my education so I could position myself to one day be in his chair, he smugly smiled and told me that I need not worry about getting additional education with Shell. If I worked hard and applied myself that would be enough. He did not know, I had researched the educational and professional backgrounds of all seven district managers within the company and all seven had Master's in Business Administration. There was only one African American who held a district manager's position. He basically was telling me I would not be a district manager, we have one of you already. I immediately set my exit plan into motion. I knew my life's work would be to help minority students attain their educational and career goals and I would be at an HBCU.

Upon leaving Shell Oil Company I took a position as an assistant coach for the Men's Basketball Team at Grambling State University. I wanted to affect young African American men and women in a positive way and help to prepare them for the rigors of higher education and corporate America. The passion I feel for this god chosen path has been truly a blessing. From an assistant coach to the Vice-President of Student Affairs/ Athletic Director over my thirty-five plus years at Grambling State University has allowed me so many opportunities to actualize my dream of making a difference in the lives of students who attended. I have worked under every president at Grambling State University with the exception of our founder, President Charles P. Adams and his successor President Ralph Emerson Jones. I have witnessed the good and the bad, the ups and the downs and I thank God for allowing me this opportunity to serve. I have seen this haven for students who otherwise would not have been afforded an opportunity to get an education, grow into an institution that is lauded around the world for its excellence,

Grambling State University, "The Place Where Everybody is Somebody!" HBCUs have made a lasting impact in my life and the lives of so many others who look like me and many who don't!

About Dr. David "Rusty" Ponton

Dr. Ponton is retired and former VP of Grambling State University. Dr. Ponton began his work at Grambling State in 1988 as an assistant men's basketball coach. During his tenure, he has also served as the head women's basketball coach, director of the Favrot Student Union, dean of student activities, dean of students, and associate vice president for student affairs. In 2016, Dr. Ponton was appointed as vice president for student affairs for the University. In addition to his higher education work, he has also worked in marketing and engineering for Fortune 1000 companies that include Shell Oil. In 2018, he also became the Athletics Director of Grambling State University Athletics Department.

Dr. Ponton's athletics higher education leadership experience began as a student at Southern University where as a student-athlete he played point-guard. He has been acknowledged for his leadership as a 2017 inductee into the Southwestern Athletic Conference Hall of Fame and an inductee into the Southern University Hall of Fame.

His athletics leadership also includes service as the Team USA Assistant Women's Basketball Coach for the R. Williams Jones Cup Team and the assistant basketball coach for the gold medal-winning Men's R. Williams Jones Cup Team for USA Basketball.

He is married to the former DeVaria Hudson of Grambling, Louisiana.

AHVERY N. THOMAS, ESQ.

I Can't Accept Not Trying

Ahvery N. Thomas, Esq.

I know it may sound cliche but "Never Give Up"! No matter what it is. Never allow yourself to think yourself out of a goal.

Being from Grambling, going to Grambling Lab, I've always wanted to run for Miss Grambling State University. Knowing many that have held the title before, I stepped on campus as a college student and I knew in my heart that goal was a destiny of mine. And I almost allowed life to derail it.

During the Spring semester of my Freshman year, election time was near. I decided that I would try my luck in running for Miss Sophomore. By this time in my matriculation, I had made plenty of friends and had true hopes of running and winning. I made sure that I had all of my plans together. I knew what I was going to wear each day. I chose a platform close to her heart of spreading school spirit and unity. You know, because I was a "Cheerleader". Get it? I knew exactly what I'd be doing each day of election week.

Election week went like this:

Day 1: Parade to kick off Election Week. This was a campus wide parade of the candidates running for any position on campus.

Day 2: Showcase of Candidates. If you were running for a queen position, this was the pageant portion of the election.

Day 3: Meet the Candidates in the Quad (I served Popeyes Chicken). On this day, every candidate would have a booth they could set up where students could come and enjoy election week, meet some candidates.

Day 4: Tiger Thursday with the Candidates. This was like Quad day, but on the yard without the food and booths. A more intimate way to meet the candidates. Last but not least

Day 5: Election Day. The day where you'd find out if you succeeded in your election.

Now back then, voting was just like any state election. We had the voting machines set up with the curtain that you close and then cast your vote. I went in and casted my vote with sincere relief that I had a good shot at this. As Election Day came to a close, all candidates, no matter what you ran for, were escorted to a room where the candidate and an extra person could go in and listen to the results as they were called out. They got to the Miss Sophomore results and I was nervous. Very nervous, so nervous that I began to sweat. Well. I'm sure you guessed it by the title of this chapter, I didn't win. I left the building and went to my car and cried. I was so hurt. I put my best foot forward, planned out everything from the food I'd give out, to my platform to better the university, to the clothes I wore each day. It wasn't enough. At that point, I told myself that I would never allow myself to be hurt in that manner ever again. At that point, running for the "Big Crown" was no longer a goal or a dream.

As I continued on in school, my family knew how much I wanted to run for Miss. Grambling State University and how long I had that dream. So, when the conversation came up during my junior year about running, imagine their surprise when I told them I no longer wanted to run and I didn't want to put that type of hurt on my heart again if I didn't win. During this conversation with my mom, dad, sister, and brother, they collectively agreed that I was talking nonsense. How could I not want to at least try something I have spoken about doing since I was in grade school. I explained the hurt I felt with running for and not winning Miss. Sophomore. That I felt, "Who am I to want to run for Miss Grambling when I could not even win Miss Sophomore?" My family stared at me as if I had lost my mind. They knew how long I had been wanting to run for Miss Grambling. My grandmother even used to call me "Queenie" because I wanted this since I was a little girl. My family fed positivity into me and let me know that losing one election does not mean the next try will have the same outcome. My family allowed me to sit and think about my decision and how I would feel if I let the opportunity pass me by. My dad made a statement that stuck with me. He said, "Now Ahvery, you are going to spend the rest of your life wondering if you had a chance to win, if you don't try." With that, I reluctantly decided to go ahead and run. However, I was still scared on the inside. But, if I was going to run for Miss. Grambling, I was going to give it all I had!

Once I made the decision to run, I had a lot of things to do. I was already late in the game and had some catching up to do. First things first, I had to get a campaign manager, someone that was well known and could hit the ground running. I called "Cousin." A person that I found at school, whom I found out was my distant cousin, so his nickname from me was "Cousin." I called and said, "Cousin, I need your help." He said, "What you need, Cousin?" I said, "I have decided to run for Miss. Grambling." He screamed in my ear, and said, I am coming right over.

At my parents' home, we started to brainstorm for the entire campaign, from my platform, to my colors, t-shirt designs, slogan, wardrobe, strategy for voting (now electronic via student emails), parade ideas, food, EVERYTHING! We had to get to rolling on everything. Next was getting my campaign team together. Once my friends and line sisters were solidified, the next issue was paying for the campaign. Don't let anyone tell you it's cheap to run a campaign, they lied. Now to pay for the campaign, you need sponsors. I wrote up my letters and sent them out to businesses, family members, and friends to see who could help out. As soon as I got my sponsors, we started to design the t-shirts, bags, pens, and anything else my mom could find on the internet that she could place my face, slogan, or name on. We got my signs printed, platform memorized, evening my gown for the showcase, whatever was needed, my team and I got it together. By the time election week started, we were a well-oiled machine.

As we candidates lined up for the "Election Week Parade of Candidates", my heart was so full at all of my friends that came in to start this journey with me. I had three black trucks filled with friends and classmates. This was actually the first time where I was completely happy with my decision to run for Miss. Grambling and my concern and worry of the thought of losing fell away from me. I knew, at that point, it did not matter if I won or lost, but what mattered was knowing that the love that was shown to me at that time was true and pure.

The week's schedule was jam packed from Monday at 5pm to Friday at 5pm, there was non-stop campaigning. Even when I went to class, I was in a campaigning mood. I would get up early to feed the athletes in the weight rooms and the early bird students going to their 8 o'clock classes. My team and I would stay up late each night planning for the next day. We had an assembly line set for everything we gave out. Whether it was gift bags, water with stickers over the labels, scantrons packets since finals were around the corner. Those who I had in my corner went far and beyond for me. I am so appreciative of those who gave me their time and patience throughout that week. They showed love that I could never pay back. At this time though, I was in a space of wanting to win, but not for me, for the team I had behind me. So, I had to finish strong.

As the week came to a close, that nervousness started to set in on me again. So much so that I opted to not even go in Grambling Hall for the reading of the results. I sat in my car with my good friend, Frank. Cousin and my mom went in for the reading of the results. As I was sitting in the car with Frank waiting, I stopped looking at my phone and turned the music off in the car. I turned the air on full blast because I was sweating. My car was parked on the side of the building. I did this because I didn't even want to see people come out of the building and be able to read the results on their faces. Yes, I was that nervous. I just needed a text of yay or nay. I never got the text. As an alternative, I got a group of my friends and family running around the corner to my car. My mom and Cousin in front and yelling "YOU WON! YOU WON!". I cried this time too. However, I cried happy tears. I got out of the car and hugged everyone I could. I saw my dad walking down the sidewalk. I ran to him yelling, "I WON!". He gave me a hug and said, "That's good Ahvery, I never doubted you."

About Ahvery N. Thomas, Esq.

Ahvery Thomas is from the small collegiate town of Grambling, La. Here, she graduated from the laboratory school. She then enrolled and graduated from the HBCU located in the same town, Grambling State University. Here is where she was elected, Miss Grambling State University, 2009-2010. She pledged the Delta Iota Chapter of Delta Sigma Theta. She graduated with a Bachelor of Science degree in Business Management and a Master of Science in Sports Administration. She then worked for a Fortune 500 company, J. P. Morgan Chase, for a year. She left that job when she was accepted into law school at Southern University Law Center. She then began to work in the Athletics Department on campus and at the Sun Belt Conference in New Orleans, La. After graduating from Law School and passing the Louisiana Bar Exam, she was promoted to the Director of NCAA Compliance and Title IX Investigator. She later started serving her community by taking a job at the Legal Services firm working with foster children. She is now a practicing attorney in the Baton Rouge area.

In her free time, she enjoys volunteering with helping feed those who are less fortunate and mentoring the youth. She also enjoys reading, writing, and spending time with family and friends.

Her aspirations in life include owning her own law firm and become a successful entrepreneur owning businesses that not only add to the economy within the community but give second chances to youth. She also wants to start a non-profit focusing on those youth in need the second chances.

Ahvery Thomas is the daughter of educators, Dr. Edwin B Thomas, Sr. and Rhonda Thomas. She has two siblings, Ahsaki Thomas and Edwin B. Thomas, Jr. She is also an Auntie to her lovely niece, Zharia Thomas.

SHONNIE MURRELL

My HBCU Experience was truly amazing!
Shonnie Murrell

Growing up, my mom owned a beauty shop by the bus station on Grambling State University's campus, and I attended Alma J. Brown Elementary that is on the campus as well.

I remember getting to meet the legendary Coach Eddie Robinson many times; he would come sit in the salon, speak words of wisdom to me, and he even told me multiple times that I am destined for greatness. One time, he gave me an autographed dollar, and, like a typical kid, I spent it at the candy store.

I even remember meeting Erykah Badu due to the fact that she hung out at my mom's salon a few times; the same could be said for actress Natalie DeSalle, actor Darius McCrary, NFL players (due to my relatives who played at Grambling were drafted into the NFL would come by along with their friends), and so many more came through my mom's hair salon.

Surrounded by greatness! I attended every homecoming I could as a kid; I loved seeing everyone on the yard, having a great time, and the world famed Tiger marching band would come through, high stepping. I wanted to be a Drum-Major instantly, and I just fell in love with the entire HBCU culture! It was even better than what I saw on *Different World* growing up!

Because I came from a family who made history at this prestigious university, I knew that I was standing on their shoulders, but I also knew that I would have to do things my own way.

My mom got married to my dad, who is truly GramFam, and we moved to Houston, TX; he became the President of the Douglas L. William chapter GUNAA later in the years

I made history at Sharpstown High School by becoming the first African-American Miss Sharpstown, an all-star athlete, the drum-major of the band, and the captain of the Drum-Line. Everyone at my school knew what university I planned to attend after graduating high school because I would frequently wear Grambling apparel. My only uncertainty was whether I would accept a scholarship through athletics or music.

One day, the legendary Dr. Edwin Thomas, of the World Famed Tiger Marching band came to Jack Yates High School to recruit students based on auditions. I was sweating bullets the entire time! He had a straight face the whole time. I ended up being a P1 which meant that I gained a full scholarship.

I arrived at Grambling at the end of July. Not only did the freshman personnel have to report on August 1st but so did the upper class-man; this was the second time in the band's history that this had ever happened.

Our first game was in San Jose, CA. We only had two weeks to learn everything. I was in overload because we were learning marching techniques, drills, cadences, dances and songs.

This is where I met my crab brothers and sisters, and those relationships are still cherished to this day; we will always be family. Life-long, lasting relationships had just begun, and I can honestly say we all still love to cut-up together!

In the World Famed, you automatically become a celebrity, and the name speaks for itself!

Literally, everywhere we would go, people of all nationalities wanted to take pictures, get autographs, and interview us.

Being on not one drum but four at one time had not ever been done by a female in the World Famed… that is, until I did it. I am honored to say that I am the first female quad/quint player for the World Famed.

Speaking of my very first half-time show, I can still vividly picture it in my mind. A sold-out game with over 60,000 people in attendance, hearing and seeing the canons blast off, seeing smoke in the air, and hearing the drum-majors whistle blows and the roar of the crowd like never before! From this very moment, I knew my life had changed for the greater.

The only way we could dominate the SWAC with Dr. Larry Pannell as the head band director, was to rehearse for long days and nights. Luckily, we also had the assistance of the all-star staff: Dr. Edwin Thomas, Mr. Charles Lacy, Mr. Malcom Spencer, and Ms. Cowan. All of them reminded me of the barbershop characters from Coming to America; there was never a dull moment with them.

I would be so exhausted after rehearsals, and I couldn't, for the life of me, figure out how my brothers and sisters had enough stamina to party. However, it made sense when I considered that they did not have to stay an extra two to three hours at practice like I did.

Being in the World Famed groomed me into the woman I am today because we traveled the world, met so many celebrities, attended an inauguration, were given the band of the universe title at the Rose Bowl Parade, were bombarded with cameras while playing, filmed major television commercials, starred in movies, and so much more.

I, also, pledged Sigma Alpha Iota Music Fraternity for Women which is an organization that promotes interaction among those who share a commitment to music.

My sisters and brothers from the World Famed are some of the most talented individuals that I have met in my life. This organization groomed me into becoming a better artist and musician, and it truly enhanced my showmanship across the board!

Joining any organization on an HBCU campus is an experience that one will take with them forever; this is especially true when everyone in your organization becomes family.

Even outside of my experiences in the band and my music fraternity, Grambling is my village.

I am blessed to say that I had relatives on campus, my godfather, Coach Rusty Ponton, took care of not just me but all students; I had Nanny Roslyn Lewis at the bookstore;I even had cousins as professors who were extra hard on me in class. Nothing was given, it had to be earned!

Whenever I needed a meal, needed to wash clothes, needed gas, etc. My GramFam was, and has always been, there for me.

I graduated with my Bachelor of Science in Business Management; I spent many nights in the College of Business at Jacob T. Stewart.

I learned a great deal from my professors, as well as from contracts, closing deals and so much more! They explained everything in detail, had patience with students, and made sure that they always helped students remain successful.

As a student in marching band, it was extremely important to stay on top of your grades, attend tutorials, turn work in early, and keep your GPA above a 3.0. It was necessary because we travel all year long.

In band, I became Freshman of the Year, Drill Sergeant second Year, and Third and Fourth year, I became Master Drill Sergeant which is the highest rank position in the band.

"Being a leader is one thing, but being a great leader is another"; this is what all of my band directors would say.

Being a part of Grambling State University history is one of the biggest blessings in my life, and I would not ever trade it for the world. It even landed me on a BET docudrama called *Season of the Tiger* which opened many doors. I have traveled the world performing, and I still do. Even some of my very own band members are World Famed, but it consists of a mixture of other HBCU bands as well.

Season of the Tiger was very exciting! I was chosen to be on the show due to my position in the band. Cameras followed me literally everywhere; everyone on campus watched me as well as rooted me on; it was an amazing feeling! From the BET awards to *106 & Park*; all of it created another kind of love that I had for my HBCU!

So, each time that I see a female in any HBCU marching band, my heart smiles. I am her, I have been her, and I know what it takes to be in a male dominated section as well as a leadership role. I love motivating the next generation to let them know that, yes, it's hard, but you can make it through, so don't you dare give up!

On Grambling's campus, I can honestly say that it really is "A Place Where Everybody is Somebody." If you go there thinking that you're not anyone, I guarantee that you will not leave this place the same.

My HBCU experience taught me about perseverance, confidence, striving for every single goal I set out for myself, knowing who it is that I am, knowing my history, and making sure that my ancestors are proud of me.

Always remember the "G" stands for "Greatness," and I wear it proudly!

About Shonnie Murrell

Known by her stage name "Shonnie" Murrell, LaShonda Antrionette Harris was born on July 19 in Jonesboro, Louisiana and raised in Houston, Texas. She has been singing and playing instruments since the age of 3.

Shonnie graduated from Sharpstown High School and received a Bachelor of Science degree in Business Management from Grambling State University. Shonnie can contribute her showmanship on percussion to her years she spent marching in the Grambling State World Famed Tiger Marching band. She is not only the first female to play Quads & Quints but she also held the highest position in the band as Master Drill Sgt. and was one of the main reality personalities on the hit BET show "Season of the Tiger". From this she landed a spot on 106 and Park, BET awards and other television appearances.

She is also a part of the Class of 2022 RECORDING ACADEMY (GRAMMYS) in which she sits on the education committee.

Funk Potion #9, which she names when performing with her full rhythm section and band, loves to give her fans the greatest performance on earth. Shonnie believes that her energy and engaging the audience are two key elements that are important to accomplish this feat! She is most of the time compared to Sheila E., Erykah Badu, and Missy Elliot because of her ability to mix her sound, lyrical, 2nd- Line, GOGO music and visual poetry all together.

Some notables that Shonnie has performed with or opened for include:

- Most recent, Percussionist for CholexHalle & Uche from American Idol at Houston Mayors Spectacular Event, Performer for Dikembe Mutumbo Congo Foundation.

- Performer for Freedom Over Texas, Head-liner for Austin Crawfish Fest, Head-liner for San Antonio, TX Mardi Gras , KPC Convention, SeerSeekers & Sundresses in Atlanta, GA

- National Anthem Singer for Rockets vs Spurs, Pelicans vs Thunder

- Cameo Real Housewives of of Atlanta, Percussionist for Legendary group SWITCH. opening act for LEELA JAMES, MAJOR., RICK ROSS, LIL WAYNE. MC LYTE, WARREN G., MACSHAWN100, LETOYA LUCKETT, ERIC ROBERSON, YOUNG JOC, the late great AL JARREAU and FRANK MCCOMB, to name a few. Her performances have taken her all over the world!

Shonnie Murrell also helps Title 1 schools (12 schools to be exact) upstart their Fine Arts programs along with her partnership with Microsoft.

RHONDA HARRIS-THOMAS

Culture Shock for This Cali Girl
Rhonda Harris-Thomas

How I got to Grambling State University to further my education may not be as interesting as some people might believe. However, it was the best decision I ever made. My mother, Sadie Harris, owned a daycare center in Los Angeles, CA. During my senior year, I was getting many offers from different colleges and universities. Some of those colleges and universities I was looking to attend were in California. At the time, I was undecided on what school I wanted to attend. My mother was close to one of the parents of the daycare and told her what I was doing. During the conversation between my mother and the parent, it was suggested that I try a college in the south because the parent said the best education in her opinion was in the south. When I talked with the parent about it, I asked her which university or college she would recommend. She said Grambling State University. I asked her what was so special about it. She said that she graduated from Grambling State University, and they had very good programs that I might be interested in. At the time I was interested in majoring in education. My plan was to get my degree in education so that I could go back home and help my mom run the daycare center.

Shortly after that conversation, I called the admissions office at Grambling to get more information. They sent me an application and everything I needed to know to enroll in school. Eventually, I was accepted to the university and was kind of excited about going to Louisiana. I wanted to attend summer school just to see how I felt about it. Little did I know, their summer school program started right after my graduation from high school. You see in Los Angeles, schools started the day after Labor Day and continued through the first week in June. Summer school at Grambling State University started the first week of June and went all the way into the first part of August. At that time summer school lasted the whole summer. Then you had two weeks off before the Fall semester started. So on my graduation night, I was not able to hang out with my classmates or go on our graduation trip to Magic Mountain in Anaheim, CA. Instead, I had to board the plane to my new adventures at Grambling State University. Then it hit me, I was heading to a school where I didn't know anybody, and I had to figure everything out by myself because I was 2,000 miles away from my mom. Being from Los Angeles, CA by the way of Seattle, WA, I did not know what was in store for me at a school in Louisiana.

Once there, I kept to myself because I didn't know what to expect. Of course, I talked to people to get where I needed to be and for help, but that was it. Believe it or not, I was very shy and intimidated when I first got there. However, I realized that my options were to sink or swim, I decided I had to swim, and navigate and adapt my way through this southern culture.

The culture in Louisiana was completely different from what I was used to in Los Angeles, CA and Seattle, WA. I met people of different backgrounds and tasted foods I never heard of. And then, there was the day I got a crash course in Southern Hospitality. See, where I was born and raised, if we don't know each other, we don't speak to each other, we don't greet each other, nothing. On the day of my crash course, I was walking in front of the café. Now, back then, during the peak hours for lunch and dinner, not only was the café packed, but the area right outside of the café was as well. The café on Grambling's campus is in the middle of the Yard and students are always congregating in this area. This was where you showed off your outfit, met up with friends, watched stroll offs, and possibly even witnessed the makings, or dismantle, of a love story. As I was walking to enter the café for dinner, I noticed there were students socializing in front of the café. A young man decided to speak to me. I saw him. I decided not to speak back. He attempted to speak to me again. And again, I ignored him. That is when he called out to me and said, "If I speak to you, the least you can do is speak back." I yelled back at him, "I don't know you!" He yelled back at me, "I don't want to marry you, I don't want you to have my kids! I was just being nice and wanted to speak, all you had to do was acknowledge me and say hi!" That is when I looked around and noticed that we were the entertainment for the day on the Yard and now I am embarrassed. I walked over to him and explained to him that "where I am from, we don't speak to people we don't know." That's when he told me that I was being uppity and rude. He then told me that I am not in the city anymore and that the culture here is to acknowledge and be respectful. He stated, "Here, everyone speaks to one another." I got quiet and walked into the café.

Even though that exchange was embarrassing, I took his advice. From that moment, whenever somebody saw and spoke to me, I made sure I acknowledged them by either speaking or waving my hand. Learning this allowed me to come out of my shell and live in the moment. Not just in college, but also in life. Learning southern hospitality has opened many networking doors that would have been closed had I kept to myself the way I was when I first got to Grambling. I was able to grow close to my roommates. They were from South Louisiana and taught me even more about the culture differences between North and South Louisiana. I was able to make friends and beautiful memories from college and further into my life. As time passed, I learned to accept the southern hospitality and adapted to the way of life of Louisiana.

Due to all the great experiences and challenges that I faced while at Grambling State University, I grew as a young lady, and I opened myself up to others. I've learned to network more and stay in contact with the lifelong friends that I met while at school. I credit Grambling State University for allowing me to meet my now husband, Dr. Edwin B. Thomas, Sr. of New Iberia, LA. Today, we have three kids Ahsaki, Ahvery, Edwin II and a granddaughter named Zharia. I am thankful that I was encouraged to attend a Historically Black College and University (HBCU). Because of the experience that Grambling State University has taught me, I believe if I had stayed and attended a college or university in California, I would not have experienced the different types of cultures that were presented to me and that allowed me to grow in such a positive way. I am grateful for the attention and the dedication of my instructors and professors who made sure that I understood and helped me complete my assignments as well as successfully guiding me to receive my Bachelor's of Science degree in Elementary Education and a Minor in Special Education. I continued my education at Grambling State University by obtaining my Masters' Degree in Education plus 30 hours. As you can see, choosing to attend Grambling State University was the best decision I ever made. If I had to do it all over again, I wouldn't change a thing.

About Rhonda Harris-Thomas

Rhonda Harris Thomas was born in Seattle, WA to Sadie Anderson Harris and L.J. Harris. She was raised in Inglewood, CA where she found her love of working with children by assisting her mother in her daycare center. Upon graduating high school, she attended Grambling State University where she met the love of her life, Dr. Edwin B Thomas, Sr. Rhonda received her Bachelor of Science degree from Grambling State University in Elementary education. She also received her Master of Science degree plus 30 hours in Special Education. Rhonda then went back to school to pursue a degree in Mass Communication where she was a featured DJ for KGRM radio on the campus of Grambling State University. She is a proud member of Delta Sigma Theta Sorority Incorporated, Grambling Alumnae Chapter, and a proud member of Tau Beta Sigma National Honorary Band Sorority Incorporated, Zeta Mu Chapter. In her spare time, Rhonda enjoys traveling, meeting new people, shopping, and learning the latest dance trends from her granddaughter. She now works as a high school special education teacher with Union Parish School Board. She is the proud mother of three children: Ahsaki, Ahvery, and Edwin II. She is also the proud Nana of her granddaughter Zharia.

DEITRICH "GENERAL MEALZ" ARMSTRONG

A Meal Ticket to Success
Deitrich "General Mealz" Armstrong

It's tightly crowded in the venue. The crowd is anticipating his next move. He climbs on top of his security guard's shoulders, and then he jumps on top of a 30-foot-tall speaker. He stands up and begins his chant

"Ohhhhh"

The Crowd Responds

"OHHHHH"

The first note to "Ruff Ryders Anthem" drops and the crowd goes berserk! The four-time Grammy Nominated Rap Star, DMX, is performing for the first time in years on Revolt TV at SXSW Music Festival, and he is killing it! Guess who was right behind him? You guessed it, me, Deitrich Armstrong aka DJ General Mealz. I had just finished DJing my opening set for YFN Lucci, and Dreezy. Here I am on stage with a Hip-Hop legend. In the same building are Cee-Lo, Big Boi from Outkast, Andre Harrell (Who discovered Diddy and Mary J. Blige), Goodie Mob, and Sway from the Sway in the Morning show. I was on stage with some of the biggest rap stars in the world, and it made me truly think about how great my career has been. Who would have thought that I started my career at a prestigious university in a small country town in Louisiana?

My first DJ gig was at Grambling State University. I was a sophomore, and I had downloaded a program to my laptop and got booked to DJ a dorm room party for $50 and a bowl of Rotel dip. I ended up being there for eight hours, and it was amazing. It was the first time I got to see people enjoy the music blends I had been preparing for months. I knew they would like it because I had tried out these same blends a few weeks ago in front of some of my band member associates, and they loved them. You see, I was a member of the World Famed Tiger Marching Band (The Baddest Band in the land). I was a member of the band for all 4 years that I attended Grambling. I was a percussionist from Texas (I graduated high school in San Antonio), and I knew all forms of music. I was trained in piano and I knew how to read music for four other instruments. Grambling was the only school I was interested in,and that was because of their band program. I saw the band play Jackson State my senior year in high school and was blown away by how hype the school was. When I became a part of the band, I felt like I became a part of a small family. On the first day of August, we started Boot Camp. We had four-a-day practices in the summer before school started for the semester. The only people on campus were us, the football team, and the cheerleaders. We were up every day at 5:00 AM and went to sleep every night at midnight. It truly made me appreciate my brothers and sisters who helped me get through those difficult, and hot, summer mornings. I'm talking about 90 degrees with a humidity of 90% by 8 am. We would wake up, take ten steps outside, and be completely drenched in sweat. It was that humid, but it was that much more energizing to be with other members of the band, experiencing it all together. Being in that band was amazing. That experience, together, allowed me to see some of the most miraculous things in life. I performed for over 70k+ people every year for the Bayou Classic in New Orleans. It was truly incredible! I saw future NFL stars Colin Kaepernick and Dez Bryant when they played Grambling in Football. I even got to perform with Hurricane Chris and Soulja Boy for a halftime show (Back then, they might as well have been Lil Baby and Drake to some of us), but none of that compares to me being a part of history. In 2009, I was a part of the band that represented the entire state of Louisiana in the inauguration for the first black president of the United States of America, Barack Obama. Every state gets one band to represent them and we were chosen for him. I'll never forget that day. It was the first time I saw what 1 million people look like, in person. It was scary, at first, but once we finally marched down Pennsylvania Avenue in DC, and we saw Barack, Sasha, Malia, and Michelle waving to us during the inauguration, it was truly one of the best experiences of my life. I will remember it forever, and I have Grambling to thank for that.

You would think with all of this partying and traveling the country with the band that I wouldn't have been able to focus in my classes, but I graduated with my Bachelor's of Science Degree in Chemistry during my 4 years there.

Yes. *That* chemistry.

It was an absolute challenge. Everyday required studying because we were, practically tested weekly in all of our classes. I had some of my hardest classes in college with advanced classes in algebra, biology, and nursing. It was beyond strenuous. I sometimes wondered what I was thinking. However, I figured it out. It allowed me to work with some of the most passionate scientists in the state. I saw people who gave their whole lives to the study of science and it was amazing. I was able to see what it looked like to have true passion for your career. It also allowed me to harness my passion into the things I love, like DJing. I was kind of forced into DJing but in a great way. You see, I had 8 AM classes every Monday, Wednesday, and Friday, and I had 5 AM lab classes on Tuesdays and Thursdays. Then, I had band class every day from 3 PM - 6:30 PM and then band practice from 8:00 PM - 10:00 PM. Therefore, I couldn't work a regular job. I had to be creative, so I started hustling with my DJing. I started spinning at parties for $50, $100, or just some food. Anything to survive, and it was working, so I decided to start promoting myself. However, I wanted to be different, so I started to pass out mixtapes for free. I used my own money, burned my own mixtapes, and passed them out on the yard, in the cafe, and in the library. They got so popular that the school started to book me for other events on campus, and that allowed me to expand off of campus where I went to Ruston, Louisiana and secured my first DJ Residency at a bar called 3 Docs Brewhouse. They were just starting and needed a good DJ for cheap. I started DJing there every Thursday - Saturday for $75 a night. It was the most money I ever made in one day so I was thrilled. They were only averaging 10 - 15 people a night there. I started putting my hustle to work, and, in 6 months time, I was DJing for 600 - 700 people every night I was there. It also forced me to not just play hip hop but to play pop music as well because 3 Docs was in between Grambling and Louisiana Tech, so both schools showed up to party every week. It was the only place where both schools showed up to party with each other every single week. By the time I graduated, I was one of the most popular DJs on campus, and It started me off on my path to greatness.

Even though my DJ Career (where I am still doing over one hundred gigs a year) is winding down, I also still own Stocks, Investments, A Vending Machine Company, and a Restaurant. My Networking and connections at Grambling allowed me to truly flourish and even give back to the school. In 2019, I flew to New York city and went on the Sway in the Morning Show on Sirius XM (the number one Hip-Hop morning show on satellite radio) and performed for over one million listeners while wearing a custom-made Grambling jersey in honor of NCAA basketball and Grambling legend, Shakyla Hill. In 2022, I donated $2000 to the Grambling drumline to cover for the expenses of their Drumheads during their performance in the Bayou Classic. I will always show love and appreciation to my prestigious institution for how they helped shape me as an overall person in the world.

Grambling State University allowed me to utilize my biggest and best strengths while also showing me how to network properly. I was able to really find myself and become the man I am today. Going from an eighteen-year-old kid who was the first in his immediate family to go to college to a grown man who owns businesses across multiple states is truly an amazing feat and I will love Grambling for the rest of my life for that.

You've got to love a coming-of-age story!

About Deitrich "General Mealz" Armstrong

Deitrich "General Mealz" Armstrong has been a staple in the entertainment business. Originally from Chicago, This Atlanta Based DJ averages over 100+ gigs Every year. He has played prestigious Festivals like A3C, LuckyFest, and SXSW. Some of his Clients are Redbull, Ice Cube's Big 3, Livenation, ESPN, and Top Golf. He has also performed for the NCAA National Championship, House of Blues, Revolt TV's Revolt House, and The Sway in the Morning Show on Sirius XM radio. He has shared the stage with Grammy Nominated artists Rick Ross & DMX, YFN Lucci, Joe Budden, and even The Late Avicii's Protege Syn Cole. In 2016, He released his first 4 track EP entitled "One" as an Independent Album Release, charting on Canadian Radio charts. With 15 years of experience as a musician, his signature style of mixes and mashups is what keeps him in high demand!

SEAN MOORE

A Pitcher's Dream

Sean Moore

"Old Grambling, dear Grambling We love thee, dear old Grambling...." Not only are these the first few words of the Grambling Alma Mater, but also words that touch my spirit every time it is sung. I owe so much to my beloved university as it played a major role in the development of who I am today. I can honestly say I have been around the Grambling culture all my life. Born the great grandson of the late, great Coach Eddie G. Robinson and having many family members attend this university such as my mother, aunt, uncle, grandparents, and cousins, I felt that attending Grambling State University was the only school for myself. I wanted to continue the legacy and walk in the footsteps of those before me. I wanted to experience all the great stories I had heard, and my time had finally come. From attending homecomings and Bayou Classics as a child and young teenager, I could only imagine how my experience would be as a proud student of the institution that dawns the colors of black and gold.

Unlike my mother and father who were from Louisiana, I was born and raised in Georgia. Born in downtown Atlanta, in the heart of the city at Georgia Baptist Medical Center and raised on the southside in Clayton County, going back to the state where my parents grew and evolved was always a thought in the back of my head. I grew up in a family where football was the main sport of interest for many, but I decided to go a different route and turned to the great sport of baseball.

Baseball had been a part of my life since the age of 6, and as my senior year of high school approached, it was time to narrow down my choices on where I wanted to further my studies upon graduation.

Grambling State University was at the top of my list. I wanted to not only attend Grambling, but I also wanted to be a part of the baseball team. As the final months of senior year had swiftly started to pass, I started to gain many college acceptances as well as opportunities to continue my athletics beyond high school. Amongst those college acceptances earned, was Grambling State University and I could not be more excited to receive this acceptance into the school that has always been a part of my life. The first half of my dream was complete by receiving this acceptance, but I still had some work to do on receiving an opportunity to continue my athletics at Grambling State University.

As my senior baseball season concluded, I received offers to play baseball at Morehouse, Clark Atlanta, and a few other HBCUs, but I had yet to receive an offer to play at Grambling State University. Through my family, I have had opportunities to develop great relationships with many different people and one relationship that I will forever be thankful for and cherish is the relationship I developed with legendary baseball coach, Wilbert Ellis. Coach Ellis was the head baseball coach at Grambling from 1977-2002 and was a dear friend of my great-grandfather, Eddie G. Robinson and our family. After the spring 2010 baseball season, Grambling baseball coach. That coach was James Cooper, a former player and protege of Coach Ellis.

It was now the summer of 2010 and I had academically committed to Grambling but knew I had the skill to also play baseball at Grambling. After a conversation with my grandfather Eddie Robinson Jr., he reached out on my behalf to Coach Ellis about my aspirations to play for Grambling. Coach Ellis was able to set up a summer workout for me to show my skills in front of Coach Cooper and his staff. Finally headed down to Grambling to showcase my skills with my mother and another family member, it was time to complete my dream and receive a scholarship offer to play for Grambling.

During the workout, I met the coaching staff at Grambling and showcased my skills on the pitching mound but sadly left the workout without a scholarship offer to play at Grambling. As days passed after my workout, and I had yet to receive the call I was looking for, I made the decision that I would try to walk-on to the baseball team, not giving up on my goal to play for Grambling. Then a few days later, I received a phone call from Coach Cooper, and it was the call that I had always dreamed of receiving. I had finally received a scholarship offer to join the Grambling baseball program and my dream was now complete.

My time at Grambling State University was full of experiences. First stepping foot on campus as a student in August of 2010, I was a young teenager from the southside of Atlanta who truly only knew 3 other Georgia students attending Grambling as well. The great grandson of Eddie G. Robinson, a legendary figure in Grambling history, is who I was, but I knew I wanted to make a name for myself by myself and not because of who I was related to.

Being a student athlete at Grambling took up much of my time. From the tempo of our first 5:30 am practices, to workouts in the weight room, and concluding with our afternoon practice, I quickly learned that collegiate baseball was entirely different from high school baseball, and it was truly a business. That scholarship that I was offered wasn't a four-year scholarship, but a scholarship that was year to year, and I had to produce each year to keep it. I played baseball and pitched at Grambling for only three years. Throughout those three years, I was able to develop a bond with many of my teammates who I call my brothers to this day. Growing up as an only child, being a part of this baseball team gave me a different type of brotherhood that I had never experienced before. GSU Baseball also gave me the opportunity to travel and visit different parts of the country that I had dreamed of seeing and I am thankful for those experiences every day.

After my 3rd year of baseball, I understood that I wasn't going to become a professional athlete and made the decision to forgo my final years of eligibility and became a regular student at Grambling. It was a hard decision to make, but it was the right decision. I retired my baseball cleats and started working in the bookstore under Ms. Nanny Ros and Mrs. Lela Buckner. These two ladies I am forever indebted to as they saw a young man with a bright future ahead of him. They helped polish me as a young adult and opened me up to a network of new opportunities daily.

My undergraduate years were finally coming to an end, and I still did not know what I wanted to do after graduating. I was receiving a degree in Marketing, but I didn't truly know what I wanted to do with that degree. After much thought and consideration, I decided to stay at Grambling for an additional two years and work towards receiving my Master's degree in Sports Administration. While working towards my second degree at Grambling, I worked at the bookstore an additional year and then had the pleasure of working on staff as a Graduate Assistant with the GSU Football Team under Head Coach Broderick Fobbs and DFO Rick Jackson. Working in sports had always been a passion of mine and being able to work for the organization where my great - grandfather played such a key role was truly an honor. As I worked in a space where I saw his pictures throughout the Stadium Support Building which stood atop of a stadium that dawned his name was very fulfilling to the heart and truly special.

Grambling provided me with different experiences that I never thought I would have in life. It has opened me to a network and put me in rooms that I could have never imagined possible. Once a dream, turned into reality, I owe so much of who I am today, to the HBCU founded in 1901 by Charles P. Adams. I left Grambling with my own legacy and not just the great grandson of "Grambling Royalty." Lifelong experiences, relationships and friendships were made in Grambling, Louisiana and for that I am forever grateful for Grambling State University.

About Sean Moore

Sean Moore was born in Atlanta, Ga and raised on the Southside Clayton County, Georgia. He went on to continue the family tradition of attending Grambling state university. While there he was a pitcher on the Tiger Baseball Team. He went on to receive his Bachelors in Marketing and Masters in Sports Administration. Upon receiving his degrees, he went back to hometown and serves as a High School College and Career advisor and athletic coach for Fulton County School district. He considers himself a sneaker and sports enthusiast.

ERIK B. JOHNSON, M.Ed.

I Didn't Choose Grambling, Grambling Chose Me
Erik B. Johnson, M.Ed.

It's surely a blessing, and indeed a treat, to be given the opportunity to share my pivotal story about Mother Grambling, and, for that, I'm forever grateful. I tend to always get pretty emotional and choked up when I sit in deep thought and reflection about how far I've come in life. I owe it all to my beloved alma mater because, without her, I can truly say that I'd be dead or back inside of a jail cell. To put it into perspective for each of you, shortly after graduating from high school, in November of 2012, I was sitting in a cell facing up to ten years in jail for living an extremely fast life at an extremely early age.

This was a very low, yet pivotal, point in my life; this is where I truly saw, first hand, the power of God and a praying mother – and, little do I know, this is what I would need the most in the season of my life where God had already ordered my steps. I'll never forget the day in December of 2012, I received a telephone call from a very close friend of the family named, U.S. Army Maj. (Ret.) Christopher Thomas who, by the way, is like an uncle to me. He stated that I crossed his mind and wanted to know if I was interested in going to school on a full ride R.O.T.C. scholarship at a university where his longtime friend U.S. Army LTC (Ret.) LaDaryl Franklin was the Professor of Military Science at the time, and my answer was an immediate no. I, honestly, had given up hope on going to school after losing the athletic scholarships and opportunities prior to my high school graduation. All I wanted to do was enlist in the army as a private and make as much money as I could, while I could. I distinctly remember sitting at the table in my parent's den with an army recruiter when my mother entered the room and handed me the phone. After I responded to Maj. Thomas, declining his offer, he then asked me once more, and, after I declined his offer for a second time, he told me it was no longer a question or a choice, but it was a direct order; anyone who knows my "Uncle" Chris, knows he can be very persistent and persuasive, if you know what I mean.

On an early Saturday morning in January of 2012, I found myself on the first greyhound bus headed to Grambling, LA, and, little did I know, my life was taking a drastic turn for the best. In that very moment, it was an indescribable feeling to have been granted a second chance at life because, to be honest, a part of me felt that leaving the state of Texas could halt the harsh reality that I once felt was setting in. However, the true reality was that I could never outrun the terrible things that I had done up to this point all I could do was pivot and turn the page and begin to write a different story. I didn't know what God was doing in this season, but I do know I didn't want Him to do it without me.

Who would've thought the kid from Dallas, TX, who rode the greyhound bus to LA, would go on to speak on the steps of the Louisiana State Capitol and on live television about the injustices and radical change that needed to be had and given to the historically black colleges and universities in the state of Louisiana? Who would've thought that the kid who graduated from Lancaster High School would go on to be a part of the Council of Student Body President's while creating and facilitating the service learning for the entire state of Louisiana's colleges and universities? Who would've thought that the kid who was facing ten years in jail would go on to be the Student Government Association President while being a pivotal part of the search committee for the next President of our beloved university? Who would've thought that the kid who used to sell drugs and carry a gun would go on to be one of the first Army ROTC Cadets to go overseas to Germany and Romania to conduct missions and build relationships with foreign military forces and diplomats? Who would've thought the kid who almost lost his life one night at a house party with one of his childhood friends would go on to graduate from undergrad as a distinguished military graduate, with 2 degrees? Who would've thought that the kid who went to jail for the first time when he was 15-years-old would go on to be named Mayor for the day in the city of Tuskegee, Alabama? Seriously, who would've thought it?

Priceless moments and experiences for some often come far and in between for others, but there's a special exception for those of us who attend Mother Grambling, for us, we get the pleasure to view and feel these priceless moments each and every day God sheds light to strike our beloved institution of higher learning. I'm forever thankful that Mr. Booker T. Washington sent Mr. Charles P. Adams to Grambling, LA where, on November 1st 1901, he would organize and establish the Colored Industrial and Agricultural School. The history is rich, our soil is the sweetest, and the fruit bearing from the trees and the labor put in by those who have come before us and will soon come after is undying and world renowned! In my opinion, this is the sweetest place on this side of heaven. This is the home of champions and unlimited tomorrows, and it's because of those unlimited tomorrows that have given kids like me the opportunity to rewrite their own respective story's and change the untimely hands of time. A happy man will go to college and obtain his degree, but a blessed man will walk the halls of GSU and not only obtain his degree but also return home as a man and the pillar of his own community, and this is truly a life worth living. Today, I stand proudly and say that I'm that man, the Grambling Man.

There's a little saying at Grambling that, "It's the place Where Everybody is Somebody," and that would go on to truly be an understatement throughout my matriculation as an undergraduate student at GSU. This is where I would go on to meet some of the greatest men and women I've met to date. It's the place where everybody truly is somebody. It's because of legends like David "Rusty" Ponton, Barbara Payne, LaTari Fleming, Sharon Perkins, Roslyn "Nanny" Lewis, Charlotte Favors, Ms. Kilgore, Ms. Collins,

Terry Lilly, Louisiana State Representatives Patrick Jefferson and Rick Gallot, Ms. Lela Buckner, Miss. Erica, Dr. Smiley, Dr. Obadiah Simmons, Dr. Carter, and so many more that the standard was set every day God gave us the opportunity to walk that great campus. We had so many great examples of what the Grambling Men and Grambling Women were supposed to, and could, be. This was more than enough to create my own opportunities for a fruitful and successful life of my own. I saw, first-hand, that obtaining a degree from this world-renowned university could take me as far as the eyes could see; I saw that anything was possible – and, for that, these great men and women will forever be etched in my heart.

After not being able to remain a successful collegiate baseball player, I sure did think that life was over for me, but Grambling State University showed me something so much more differently. This is why, when asked about my story, I'm sure to place this illustrious institution of higher learning at the forefront of my success and list it as a pivotal ingredient to the radical change that has happened in my life. I gained a lifetime bond and friendship with people from all walks of life; I gained so many family members who still, after eight years of being removed from undergrad, still celebrate each other's wins the same way we did when we once walked that very campus. Again, I didn't choose Grambling, Grambling chose me – and, to this very day, it's one of the greatest things that's ever happened to me. I'm forever grateful for that Saturday afternoon in December of 2012 where my mother came and handed me the phone, and it was my Uncle Chris on the other line. I can't wait to share this story with my children, and, if I'm lucky, they too will go on to be prestigious Grambling Men and Women.

About Erik B. Johnson, M.Ed.

Erik B. Johnson, M.Ed., is a former active-duty 1st Lieutenant in the United States army where he served his country for 8 years. Throughout his time in the army, he served as a Platoon Leader, Combat Scout and Executive Officer wanted to serve his community in another capacity through education and involvement to empower the next generation of young leaders. Shortly after exiting the military in October of 2017, Erik began working in the medical field while completing his teacher certification. Erik is now a special education teacher, behavior intervention coordinator and Varsity athletic coach in Desoto ISD. Erik has an undying passion for helping those who cannot help themselves. He proudly accepts the challenge of reaching those who have been written off by others and those who cannot properly advocate for themselves both in and out of the educational setting. Currently in his fifth year of teaching and coaching, Erik is truly living in his passion and walking on God's word.

Shortly after receiving his high school diploma from Lancaster High School in 2011, Erik enrolled in Grambling State University in January 2012 where he would begin matriculating as a double major In Kinesiology and Mass Communications. While attending his beloved alma mater, Erik would hold key positions as Student Government Association President (SGA), SGA Junior Class Vice President, a Senior Leader with the Student Ambassador Associations, on-air radio personality with the KGRM radio network, cadet command sergeant major and ranger challenge team co-captain in the GSU Army ROTC Tiger Battalion, just to name a few. In August 2021, Erik received his Master's of Education in Educational Leadership and Policy Studies with a principal certification from University of Texas – at Arlington. Erik plans to start his journey of obtaining his Doctorate of Education at the University of Southern

California. Erik is a proud member of Alpha Phi Alpha Fraternity, Inc., Cedars of Lebanon #21 Masonic Lounge, The Genesis Chapter of United Afrikan American Men, Inc. (U.A.A.M.), Sigma Alpha Pi National Leadership Honor Society, Grambling's National Alumni Association (GUNNA), and the Texas High School Coaches Association (THSCA).

Above all, Erik acknowledges none of this would be possible without his Lord and Savior Jesus Christ and his loving parents Myran and Danny Johnson Sr. It is with his upbringing by his parents, grandparents Dorothy Louise Brisco, Claude William Roddy Jr., Bennie Grace Johnson, and Claude Jefferson Duke that propelled him to reach the highest of heights. Erik is constantly motivated by his brothers Danny Johnson Jr and Kristopher Claude Johnson; it is for these loving individuals that Erik credits for his work ethic, drive, ambition, and continuous success; for it truly took a village - but most importantly this village.

Erik currently resides in Dallas, TX.

BURGUNDY C. HAMMOND-MITCHELL, ESQ.

RENT IS DUE

Burgundy C. Hammond-Mitchell, Esq.

Warning: It will evoke joy and dance with doubt. It will garner support and engage critics. It will demand lengthy days and steal endless nights. It will pay you in courage and battle with fear. That is the cost of success.

> *"Success is never owned; it is only rented —*
> *and the rent is due every day."*
>
> –RORY VADEN

Most people desire success, but few are disciplined to stay the course. Whether it's accomplishing a weight loss goal, receiving a promotion at work, or acing that dreaded final, we all crave the sense of peace and happiness that comes with success.

In my twenty-nine years, I have learned to always put my all on the line and leave nothing for tomorrow. I've applied this mantra to each and every test, goal, mistake, opportunity, failure, and decision I've faced, and I rest comfortably that I have no regrets.

Growing up in the quaint town of Alexandria, Louisiana, affectionately known by its citizens as "Alec," I knew that I wanted "more." I wanted to be successful. What would this "more" require? How would I get to this "more"? Was I capable of this "more," and who would help me achieve it?

I remember this day like it was yesterday. I was sitting outside on the newly poured concrete benches of Peabody Magnet High School. It's not long after I sat down when a bold, red, shiny, new, convertible top Chrysler 200, detailed with a Grambling State University license plate, entered the parking lot. I observed a tall, well dressed, attractive woman exit the vehicle.

At the tender age of seventeen, and having been raised by a single maternal grandmother, I wasn't exposed to much black excellence because our surroundings lacked such displays. I lived in what is referred to as "Lower Third." The negative connotation of "lower" was intentional and spoke more to the town's classification of its constituents than to indicate its geographical position. It was not a desirable part of town, and our crime rates were on a steady incline. When you're seventeen years old and a first-generation college graduate, you're not as accustomed to people that look like you having more than just enough. Seeing this woman with natural-styled hair, driving this fancy car, and pulling up to my school was my awakening.

I would go on to see this woman quite often, and, on most of those occasions, she would be adorned with black and gold GSU paraphernalia. I was immediately captivated by the pride and power she exuded. She had it. She had "more," and I wanted it too.

Fate would have it that I would go on to meet this woman who would pour her love for Grambling State University into me through scholarships and mentorship. She always accredited her success to Grambling State University. I had never even considered attending an HBCU, nor did I understand its value.

Sadly, my grandmother passed shortly before my high school graduation, and, as a result of her abrupt passing, I considered enrolling into a local college because I wanted to remain closer to my siblings, but God had different plans. Attorney Johnson promised that a tour of her beloved Alma Mater promised to be a good time, and she wasted no time in making accommodations for my tour. I didn't know the intricate details of the twists and turns that laid ahead, but God knew my next stop was Exit 81. "More" was waiting for me at Grambling State University.

For me, I knew, from the very moment my feet touched the pavement, that I was home. I had anxiously awaited High School Day for months. Grambling has that charm about her, and, if you allow her; you will find that she's chosen you long before you've chosen her. It's that feeling you get when you test drive your dream car or meet the love of your life. When you know; you just know.

To pick an isolated, life-altering moment or experience that Grambling State University has afforded me proves to be a laborious task. It simply cannot be summarized in one chapter. What I can say is that Grambling State University provided me with life-long friends, allowed me to board my first commercial flight at the age of 21, nurtured my timidity, equipped me with knowledge, granted me the ability to attend the inauguration parade of the first black President of the United States, challenged my doubts, grew my faith, and instilled patience (if you've ever been through the registration process: then you too have learned this lesson). Grambling expanded my vision of what "more" could look like for me and outlined the blueprint of how I would obtain it. I was surrounded by black excellence everywhere. From the professors and students to the visiting speakers and administration; I was intrigued with their mere existence. Life is funny like that. Sometimes you have to see it to believe it, and I was sold.

I have danced in the Black and Gold Room and strolled in the Assembly Center. I gained the "freshman 15" courtesy of the fried fish and lasagna at Cash Street and sweated to the beat of the infamous Terry Lilly aerobics. I met students from around the world and ran to Tiger Tuesday's on the Yard (seriously, who was going to miss DJ Twins and P-Skillz???). I have enjoyed countless homecomings and improved recruitment strategies.

Truth be told, Grambling State University is the very seed of my success. Every single accomplishment is just part of my harvest, declaring the manifestation of my seed. Those four years were quite possibly the best four years of my young adult life. Thank you

Grambling for everything. Thank you for producing the doctors, nurses, scientists, attorneys, politicians, judges, educators, and innovators our black and brown children need to see. Thank you for providing an atmosphere of love, equality, and independence.

Thank you for the realization that I, too, am worthy and capable of "more." Thank you for the reinforcement that our dreams are meant to be limitless, wild, and courageous. The work must continue. We must continue to donate. Continue to recruit. Continue to support and continue to protect our beloved institution. Thank you for teaching us that our work doesn't end at graduation, and that, as we travel through our own life's purpose, we all must pay the tolls. Success is not owned, and now the rent is due.

About Burgundy C. Hammond-Mitchell, Esq.

Associate Attorney at Clayton, Fruge, Ward, & Hendry Law Firm
2019- present

Sparked by a passion for justice and a genuine love for people, Burgundy knew her life's purpose would not be fulfilled until she joined the crusade against injustices for all. Today, Burgundy zealously represents clients who have been severely injured in motor vehicle accidents and have entrusted her to fight for them.

Burgundy is a proud native of Alexandria, Louisiana, the same city that continuously reaffirms her belief in the adage that "it takes a village to raise a child". Burgundy credits much of her success to the overwhelming support that she has received from the family, friends, and fellow Warhorses, in her beloved hometown.

As a true Gramblinite, Burgundy's heart bleeds black and gold, as Grambling State University is the institution that provided the pivotal foundation for her career aspirations. She is also a proud graduate of Southern University Law Center, which quickly catapulted her into the manifestation of her dreams.

Burgundy is a member of Delta Sigma Theta Sorority, Inc., the Baton Rouge Bar Association, Family Section of the BRBA, Louisiana State Bar Association, and the Young Lawyer Division of the LSBA. In 2020, Burgundy also began practicing family law which is an area that is near and dear to her heart as she was reared by a single grandmother. When she is not vigorously advocating for her clients, Burgundy enjoys quality time and traveling the world with her husband, Demario Mitchell and their beloved daughter, Teigan Mitchell.

RYAN L. WILLIAMS

Quitting is Never an Option
Ryan L. Williams

After my first year of college, and finally getting adjusted to college life in my second year, I still had no real direction or focus for my life. I grew up in the MLK neighborhood, and that shaped me personally; my community impacted me heavily. The neighborhood made me. I attribute my strength to a variety of different characteristics, including how I learned as a child. If you don't know, the MLK neighborhood, also referred to as Cooper Road, has all school levels and a college within one community: four elementary schools, Linear middle school, Green Oaks high school, and Southern University.

This environment on Cooper Road gave me a good vision of how important community and continuity is in a young life. I started school with six of my high-school classmates who were also teammates of mine. They were no longer students after our first semester of college and had moved back to our hometown of Shreveport, LA. After that first semester, I felt alone and confused. I called home to my mother to express my frustration and willingness to come home. My mother was stern, and I knew she loved me; however, her love for me wouldn't allow me to quit. Her rule was always that if you start something, you better finish it. I grew up in a family where that was frowned upon simply because it's up to you to know who you are.

For those people who don't believe in you, prove them wrong through your actions. I have worked tirelessly to be the best possible person I can be. It hasn't always been perfect, but each lesson has been a worthy one despite the challenges I have faced. I'm from one of the most dangerous places in Shreveport, but I made it simply by staying focused and continuing to believe in myself.

When I got to Grambling, I didn't really have any direction; I just knew that, if I graduated, my life would be somewhat better than those who didn't. My mother was a seventeen-year-old, pregnant, high school dropout who went back to school and became a nurse; she understood the importance of an education. I stayed at school, bitter but determined.

It was my second semester of my second year when, one day, my cell phone rang, and it was a girl who I had an encounter with during the previous semester of my second year. She had a son, and she was letting me know that I may be the child's father. I was just adjusting to school and school life; I wasn't ready to be a father. I told my mother that I wanted to drop out of school to get a job, so I could take care of my son; she told me that it's going to be difficult going to school and having the responsibility of raising a child, but that I couldn't quit school, and she would do whatever she had to do to help me not only be a good father but a good student.

I took a paternity test to find out that I was, indeed, the father of a boy whose mother named him Jordan. She had moved to Mississippi with her parents, and they were helping her raise her son. I met Jordan for the first time that semester. That meeting changed my outlook on life. From that moment on, I knew I wanted to be better for him. I knew that I wanted to do any and everything I could to make him proud. He became my primary focus.

Jordan would stay with me in the summers at my mom's house and sometimes in my dorm room when school was in session. It was a six hour ride each time to pick him up for holidays and breaks. Jordan watched my struggles and my progress. He saw me graduate from college twice, serve my country in the USAF, and start several multimillion-dollar businesses. My goal was to make him proud and have him know that quitting is never an option. In the fall of 2023, exactly twenty years after I became a freshman at Grambling State University, I dropped my son off at Grambling State University as a freshman. I'm not sure what his experiences will be like, but I do know one thing: quitting is not an option.

Grambling State University afforded me the opportunity and allowed me a chance to grow as a person and as a man. The personal relationships and friendships are everlasting. My matriculation allowed me to compete on all levels. The proudest of times is being in the U.S Air Force and being able to stand alongside others from around the world as a graduate of Grambling proving that I'm worthy and able to do things just as well as others. I'm forever grateful for all that was invested in me.

My greatest accomplishment is being able to live out my dreams and helping others as the chief executive officer of Seedlinks Behavior Management. Seedlinks LLC is doing just that – in March I relocated my business to Marshall Street and put a ton of work into fixing the 1533 Marshall St. building. My goal was to highlight the principles that I used in order to inspire and educate. My passion to see people empowered through habits of healthy thinking became the most important story. I wanted to help young people grow up into strong men and women; when I taught school, I enjoyed the work but realized I had some limitations for how I could help. I started Seedlinks so that I wouldn't have to limit my influence because, as a teacher, I was limited to the actual coursework and class time; omitted were the other issues in a young person's personal life outside of school that affected all areas of life.

Two conversations led me to start my own business: one conversation with my mom and a second with a young kid about mental health issues and how to overcome it with the regular dosage of Organic CBD drugs. It was through these interactions that I decided to start Seedlinks Behavior management. My business started out small in 2016, with an emphasis on delivering professional care in a timely manner, and it has slowly grown into the business it is today. Now, I own a 60-70 employee firm that serves over 700 clients. I've been helping young people and adults at several locations including Ruston and Shreveport.

Seedlinks LLC is a behavioral management company that provides a variety of mental health, crisis intervention, and family stability services. Beyond treatment, we also focus on prevention measures as well as increasing access to those who might not be able to reach these services. We pride ourselves in the ability to respond to clients the same day help is needed.

Our logo is a tree, signifying the growth and change we all experience in life. A tree has a very small beginning – it starts as just a seed, yet, upon maturity, grows into something much larger, providing nourishment and shade to those around it. My business may be providing that fruit now, but the seeds and roots of that vision started long ago and took time to mature into the business we see today.

My fraternal bond has also given me heavy insight into what it really means to be an achiever. Kappa Alpha Psi was founded January 5th, 1911 in Bloomington, Indiana, and, since its conception, it has proven to be the epitome of black male excellence. I have been a member for eleven years, and my biggest accomplishment, besides being elected polemarch, was starting the Kappa League for my chapter. Kappa League is a subset of the Guide Right, our National Service Initiative. It's the premier Social Action Program responsible for training young men; it was designed to help them grow, receive, and develop their leadership talents in every phase of human endeavors. It provides both challenging and rewarding experiences, which richly enhance their lives. Membership was open to male students from 9th through the twelfth grades. The goal is to help these young men to achieve worthy goals for themselves and make constructive contributions to their community when leadership roles become the responsibility. I'm personally responsible for sending over seventy-five young men to college through this program.

Life is not how you start, but it's about how you finish, and, in the meantime, you find things that motivate you and push you to places you could only dream of. I often think, "what if I had quit when the odds were against me? Where would I be and what would my life be like?" I'm sure it would be much different; the fortunate part is I will never get to know. I'm grateful for the chances that were afforded to me and all the people who made a difference in my life.

About Ryan L. Williams

Ryan L. Williams was born July 2nd, 1984, to James and Marilyn Williams. Mr. Williams received his high school diploma from Green Oaks high school where he was a standout Football and basketball player. After high school he decided to attend Grambling State University Majoring in Political Science Pre-law where he was extremely active on campus joining many clubs and organizations where he would establish lifelong connections and meet friends who are now more like siblings. After Graduating in the fall of 2007, he decided to serve his country in the United States Airforce with the 4th Fighter wing supporting missions in Afghanistan and Iraq being honorable discharged after 4 years of service. In 2011 he decided to futher his education by attending Louisiana Tech University Graduating with a degree in Human services and Counseling. Ryan Williams now holds the title of CEO for several multimillion-dollar companies including Seedlinks Behavior Management, Redwood Property Management, Magnolia Transportation, Seeds in Action, The Beyond Beleaf Foundation and Uptown Bar & Lounge. Ryan takes pride in being an activist in the city of Shreveport & investing in his local community, youth, and those in need. He has served his community by being a part of Mayor Adrian Perkins Economic development team, Shreveport Leadership Class, member of Kappa Alpha Psi. Inc. Life Member of Kappa Alpha Psi, Inc. Shreveport Leadership Class 2020, Lead Louisiana Leadership Class Kappa League Guide right director of Kappa Alpha Psi. INC.A 15000.00 Endowment to Grambling State University providing scholarship to students of Booker T. Washington & Green Oaks High schools and is currently the Polemarch for The Bossier City Alumni Chapter of Kappa Alpha Psi, Inc. He spends his free time being a father to his children (Jordan a freshman at Grambling state university) kylon kamryn Ryan ll and kayci and adding to his car collection of over 10 classic cars. His motto in life is molded by a Quote by Dr. Martin Luther King, Jr. "NOT ALL MEN CAN BE FAMOUS BUT ALL MEN CAN BE GREAT, GREAT MEN ARE MEASURED BY THERE SERVICE"

AWARDS: Emerging business of the year, 40 under 40, Athena Award, Public Citizen of the year, Humanitarian of the year, Pan-Hellenic Council Mover and Shaker, King 19 of The Krewe of Harambee, Yokem Toyota Hometown Hero

EBONY L. GOURRIER, LCSW-BACS

Where Everybody Is Somebody
Ebony L. Gourrier, LCSW-BACS

The Grambling State University, Home of The Tigers, "Where everybody is somebody," also known as my second home. My experience at Grambling State University has impacted me in such an unmeasurable way. The value of attending a HBCU is incomparable.

I remember attending Grambling's High School Day where students from all over the world were invited to tour the university, attend a pep rally, and a football game. It was at this time I fell in love with Grambling State University. Seeing my people hold the Grambling culture in such high regard made me want to be a part of that legacy. I was convinced and convicted.

I can recall my first day of Welcome Week, a week of events curated specifically for the new incoming class. During this week, freshmen are invited to move-in a week before the rest of the students. This week included fun and educational events such as a block party, pinning ceremony, comedy show, spirit rally, Louisiana food tasting, and more.

I remember it like yesterday, it's a Sunday morning and I am accompanied by my mother and my younger brother Kamani for "Move-in Day". We were immediately greeted by members of Alpha Phi Alpha Fraternity. They welcomed us to Grambling State University and offered to assist in moving our things into the dorm. I remember them being perfect gentlemen and volunteering all morning and afternoon to help the new freshman class move in.

Later that night my roommate Schyler and I attended the first event to kick off Welcome Week, a block party! I remember us having so much fun. The DJ's were playing music from all over, so every student could "rep" where they were from. It was such a good time yall and it was just the beginning.

During my time at Grambling I joined The Society of Distinguished Black Women, also known as "DBW". The Society of Distinguished Black Women strives to maintain unity in the Black Community as well as the Black family; promoting community service and political awareness, all while emphasizing sisterhood. DBW is passionate about promoting self-esteem and self-worth. My experience with DBW was vital to my personal development and I gained women who I can call sisters for the rest of my life.

What makes Grambling great is the history behind it. Grambling is undoubtedly a family school, hence our beloved phrase #GramFam. If one were to take a poll, you'll find that more than half of Grambling students and alumni have a family member that has attended or graduated from Grambling.

We don't say GramFam because it is cute or because it rhymes. We say it because we are truly a family. HBCUs are tight knit communities and are a home away from home. It is a big family and family looks out for each other. Grambling has a club or organization for just about anything ranging from modeling troupes, book clubs, honor societies, Mental Health Club, to international student organizations, and more. This is beneficial because it shows that everyone has a place and if we did not identify with an organization, we were encouraged to create one. During my time at Grambling I met students from all around the world. Although HBCUs are a hub for black culture, all cultures are celebrated.

The value of attending an HBCU is unmatched. It is a significant impact to be surrounded and educated by successful people who look like you and share a similar cultural background.

As a graduate of one of the best HBCUs in the world, The Grambling State University, your professors teach more than what's on the course syllabus. At Grambling the professors actually took the time out to know my name and my goals. You are not treated like an additional number on a roll or another paper that a professor has to grade.

The people will pour into you like none other. There is always someone who can compensate where you lack. There is always someone who can turn your weaknesses into strengths and that is what makes an HBCU great. They care about you as a person. If you miss a few days at a HBCU they are going to call you and see what's going on.

The pride you feel in graduating from an HBCU is unparalleled. That is why we go so hard for our colleges and universities. The sense of belonging and community you inherit at Grambling is so genuine that I can call any Grambling alumni association in any state and be treated like family.

One of my most memorable experiences while at Grambling was being a part of the #HBCUsForObama movement. I along with many other students at Grambling State University volunteered to not only spread awareness of how our votes matter but also assist students in getting registered to vote in Louisiana. We also provided transportation via student shuttle buses to voting sites as well as gifted students with a t-shirt and pin to show appreciation for their contribution to society. On election day, SGA hosted a watch party and the sense of pride in the room knowing we contributed to the first African American President being re-elected was truly a moment in time.

I love Grambling and it was important to me to make an impact for future generations of Gramblinites. Throughout my time at Grambling, I served on the Student Government Association as an elected representative of the GSU student body. My roles included associate justice, class senator, and study body vice president. During my time I along with other students were essential in the passing of bills such as the Intramurals/Pool Renovation Fee, Choir Fee, Marching Band Fee, Athletic Fee, Recycling Fee, and Cheerleaders Fee. As of 2023, these student self-assessed fees are still making an impact for the current generation.

I also worked with the Information Technology Center as well as other members of SGA to install charging table tops stations that can be seen today around Grambling's campus in places such as the Tiger express, Charles P Adams, Assembly Center, and more.

At Grambling State University, I was taught I was valuable. I was taught that the things mainstream society would use against me was to be celebrated. It was at Grambling that I truly learned how to be self-sufficient. It was at Grambling that I grew from a teenager to a young woman. It was at Grambling that I learned "We do not grow in isolation, but we grow in community." It was also at Grambling State University that I met my husband and the father of my child, Leo. I am forever grateful for my experiences and knowledge gained from attending this illustrious institution. I love my HBCU! Forever #GramFam.

About Ebony L. Gourrier, LCSW-BACS

Ebony Gourrier, LCSW is a native of Shreveport, Louisiana and a proud honor graduate of The Grambling State University. Ebony is the Founder and CEO of The Lab Personal and Professional Development Center. Ebony began her career providing intensive mental health services for at-risk youth and their families. Since then, she has served as a program manager and provided clinical evidenced based treatment to military service members. In her various roles, Ebony has served as a member of the Diversity and Inclusion Board, Disaster Mental Health Team, Master Resilience Trainer, as well as provided transition assistance to servicemembers retiring/separating, and facilitating suicide prevention and sexual assault awareness trainings. As a clinician, Ebony is passionate about enhancing personal and professional development within her community, instilling resilience, as well as advocating for others. Ebony credits her success to her mother's will and God's amazing grace.

DESIREE' C. COTTON-TURNER, ESQ.

You Can't Be Great Without The G
Desiree' C. Cotton-Turner, Esq.

"30… 300… 3000… but not 3." My mother told me when I was a junior in High School that when it came to choosing where I would further my education, I could go 30 miles, 300 miles, or 3000, but I could not go 3. Many people inquire why. My mom has always been my biggest supporter, role model, and influence on my life. Everything she was, I wanted to be as well. She always encouraged me to go out into the world, see it myself, and effect positive change. She believed that travel and experience were the best teachers a young woman could have. She enormously influenced my decision on where I would further my education. She did not care where I went or how far; her only request was that I not go 3 miles.

I am a Louisiana native, born and raised in Monroe, LA. Monroe is a small rural city, with its own university, where many of my family members attended, including my mother. It is conveniently located just 3 miles from my childhood home's front door. While I always wanted to be like my mom, my mom, in mom fashion, wanted more for me and pushed me to go further than she did. I even tried to make every argument for attending her alma mater, but she always said, "30… 300… 3000 but not 3." Hindsight being 20/20, I am thankful that instead of going 3, I went 44, to be exact, to Grambling State University.

My path to Grambling State University differs from a typical one paved with family legacy, tradition, and pride. I did not have an innate love for this great institution because it was the institution that my parents met and their parents before them, and so forth. I remember passing Exit 81, traveling with my family, and never wondering what could be hiding in those rolling piney hills. Only when my mom started tailgating did I hear of Grambling, LA, let alone Grambling State University. I was impacted indirectly by many close family friends who had that innate love and pride imprinted on me. One such person was Gilbert Williams. Mr. Williams was a close family friend, and his passion for Grambling State University ran deep with him and his family. It was so intense that it was tangible. Unfortunately, he passed away before he could see me set foot on his beloved alma mater's grounds. However, I was honored to be the first recipient of his inaugural memorial scholarship when I graduated from high school in 2006.

My first personal experience of GSU was not going to a game or college fair; it was through a person, Mrs. Diane Maroney-Grigsby. While my bio says I am a passionate advocate of the law, the law was not my first love. My first love is dance and the budding ballerina that I was with the hunger to grow as a dancer. I took numerous classes in a local dance studio during the school year and summer. During my first summer intensive workshop with the Twin City Ballet, I would encounter Ms. Maroney, or as I would grow to call her, "Mama Lump," at the University I could not attend. At this workshop, my life changed by taking my first Horton class with Ms. Maroney. She would expand my passion and knowledge and impact my decision to attend Grambling. After that class, I was determined to continue to learn from her and eventually dance for her and the Orchesis Dance Company. My relationship with this phenomenal woman helped teach me the very discipline I would need to conquer law school and become a lawyer. My time under her tutelage taught me grit, determination, and discipline. The long hours on the Marley (the dance floor) would give me the agility to excel both on the stage and in the classroom.

Growing up in Monroe, I grew up in the shadow of my mom's "notoriety" as a history maker. I grew up under that identity. I had to carry myself a certain way because I was "Judi's daughter" or "Little Cotton." While it granted me certain privileges, advantages, and opportunities, that was a significant part of my identity. Traveling just 44 miles away, I developed my sense of self. I made moves that did not pan out the way I hoped, mainly my campaign for Miss Grambling, but even in loss, I gained so much. I learned that to get ahead, you must put yourself out there. Grambling taught me how to make friends and a name for myself on my merit and not on the coattails of my family name. I am proud to be a part of the "old gram," I came to Grambling in the transition phase before the new library and natatorium. I practiced sharing space with Terry Lily and the cheerleaders in the Women's Gym. I had some of the best times at Grambling State University. Where else can a blackout become a block party?

While Grambling is not the most prominent school in the state or country, its legacy and reach surmounts schools that are double and triple its size. Stepping foot on the campus for the first time as a student was electrifying. My world doubled, and I met many interesting and dynamic people. My professors and classmates impressed upon me the necessity of being open-minded. I learned so much about myself both in the classroom and out. Living on my own for the first time, not only an adjustment but my first lesson on what it meant to be accountable for my actions. I learned of Southern University and the Law Center because of Grambling State University. My career and future were shaped and molded at the place where "Everybody is Somebody", Grambling State University. The knowledge and skills I received there are invaluable. I carry many of them with me today. As I always say, you can't be GREAT without the G.

About Desiree' C. Cotton-Turner, Esq.

Desireé C. Cotton-Turner, Esq is the founding and managing attorney of DC Strategic Consulting, LLC, and Contract Attorney with the East Baton Rouge Parish Public Defender's Office. Desireé is dedicated to the integrity and professionalism of the legal system and providing clients with much-needed education on the law and legal system. Desireé prides herself on providing her clients with platinum service with legal counsel, advocacy, or consulting services. Desireé is a compassionate and zealous advocate for her clients. In addition to being a practicing attorney, Desireé is a certified mediator and Notary Public. Desireé, a Monroe, LA native, holds a BA in English from Grambling State University and a Juris Doctorate from Southern University Law Center.

JORDAN F. HARVEY

The Experience of Everything Black
Jordan F. Harvey

The question of whether to attend an HBCU had gone out of the window by age 5. It is important to note despite my awareness of other HBCUs throughout Georgia and the South, I knew I was destined to be a Gramblinite. I don't think my step-father or brothers would have had it any other way. Although thoroughly immersed in HBCU culture through the efforts and devotion of my stepfather, Marc, and my mama, Joan, my transition from Mary Persons High School in Georgia to Grambling State University in Louisiana still came with its culture shock and eye-opening experiences. Coming from a family that is full of educators and prides itself on education, I was fortunate enough to be exposed to various levels of education throughout my life, black educators, black leaders, and to be enrolled in Advanced Placement (AP) courses throughout my high school career.

Picture this, a small town in middle Georgia with one high school where everybody knows everybody (because half of us are kin), and all of us are at Dan Pitts Stadium for Friday Night Lights. The school district and county are about 60/40 white and black with the Caucasian population being the majority. This played a role in shaping me, as I was one of the only people of color in Gifted or AP classes. As well as me also being exposed to HBCUs outside of the school grind. This dichotomy set the stage and context for how transitioning from being barely represented in grade school to being celebrated and accepted university/conference wide in college. It is not as if my high school experience was plagued by racism or that the people were of lesser character, it is simply that Grambling provided a safe haven for me to learn about myself, the roots and stories of others that look like me, and to witness everything Black.

This fact and the space Grambling provided would ultimately shape many years of growth, self-love, pride, knowledge, and relationships I cherish every day. Grambling is not only where I obtained my degree in Computer Information Systems (CIS) but it is also where I learned how to draft my resume and create an elevator pitch as a freshman and member of the Alpha Tau Chapter of Phi Beta Lambda Business Fraternity. I was exposed to the power the voice of the people has through activism and being involved through the efforts of members of the Student Government Association (SGA). Learning the ropes of hospitality, organization, respect for others, and the hard work of event planning through my time on the Favrot Student Union Board (FSUB) would position me for additional tasks in my professional life at Accenture. The inherent beauty, exposure of black history and style witnessed while at Grambling by beautiful Black Queens and Kings of Grambling was a new experience and truly a breath of fresh air. It instilled joy in me and gave me confidence for life. Grambling being the place, "Where Everybody Is Somebody! ... (with a Fee Sheet)" summarizes the many spaces Grambling provides for people around the world to share and express their culture(s) while also providing "domestic" students with the space to have pride in their home states as I did with the East Coast Coalition and the Georgia Club. The array of clubs, Sororities, Fraternities, and other social groups at Grambling provides opportunities to meet friends and family for life as I have been a brother of the Gamma Gamma Chapter of Omega Psi Phi Fraternity Inc.

Referencing these extracurricular activities highlights the love and space for growth Grambling provided me throughout my journey. My growth also took place in the classroom. I was no longer embarrassed to ask questions or admit not understanding, because I was no longer in my head about how my non-Black friends or teachers would perceive me. From the classroom in Georgia where I was one of two or three other black people to being in a classroom where 98% or more are black reshaped my goals. Being a person of color and seeing "Black Excellence " or   any of our personal goals exemplified by someone who looks like us, breathes power and confidence in the next generation – it did for me. While navigating this thing called life, it helps to be seen and heard and I found the space and voice for that while at the G. Grambling presented me with many revelations about what it is to be Black that I treat as a gift, and I believe all HBCUs offer this as an undervalued asset inherent to the HBCU experience. My love for Grambling started young but the firsthand memories and people I was able to meet has taken my love, gratitude, and push for others to have the HBCU experience to new heights. Everyone's HBCU experience is different, even when there is overlap or similar themes repeated throughout, the beauty is in what experiences we have individually and how they can shape the collective.

Education is the purpose of pursuing any higher or continuing education and the education provided at Grambling was top tier. I advocate for Grambling and HBCUs not ONLY because of the education but because of the invaluable lessons you get outside of which degree program you matriculate through. A major lesson I learned was the value of relationships and the benefits of failing. I experienced a lot of success while at Grambling but often people only see what we want them to. The other side of the coin was filled with shortcomings and disappointments, some of which were self-inflicted and others which were just the highs and lows of life. The benefit of having supportive, equally ambitious, and culturally diverse friends allowed me to overcome failures and reach a lot of the success I experienced.

Education can now be obtained virtually but the opportunity to be cherished as a student and loved for who you are compared to being another number at a predominantly white institution (PWI) or online institute diminishes greatly. As a current government contractor, I can attest to the opportunities to gain certifications, additional degree programs from any and all universities but how the HBCU experience is unique and irreplaceable. I can also attest to the need for all HBCU alum to share their stories and work to continue the mission of our respective HBCUs. To this end, my brother Caesar (who is also a Gramblinite) and I partnered with our cousins to co-found the Harvey-Wilder Scholarship Foundation, a HBCU scholarship foundation dedicated to providing incoming freshmen with tuition assistance and mentorship. Our goal is to increase HBCU awareness and help those in need by reducing financial barriers of higher education at HBCUs. Through the scholarship foundation we carry the torch that my stepfather Marcus Whitehead lit and used to mentor, inspire, and provide for others.

About Jordan F. Harvey

Jordan F. Harvey was born in Forsyth, Georgia. Raised by his mother Joan Whitehead and late-stepfather, Marcus Whitehead, he was introduced to HBCUs at a very young age. His first Bayou Classic experience was in 1995 followed by countless Atlanta Classic games between Florida A&M University and Tennessee State University, Fort Valley State Homecomings, and Honda Battle of the Bands. This early and continued exposure to Historically Black Colleges & Universities helped mold his love and appreciation for our HBCUs. He graduated from Mary Persons High School in 2010 where he played football and ran track and field.

While at Grambling State University, Jordan studied Computer Information Systems (CIS) and minored in Business Management. He was actively involved in various student organizations including being a Fall 2010 initiate of the Alpha Tau Chapter of Phi Beta Lambda Business Fraternity Incorporated, Black Dynasty, BEEP, the Favrot Student Union Board (FSUB), the East Coast Coalition, the Georgia Club, a Fall 2012 initiate of the Gamma Gamma Chapter of Omega Psi Phi Fraternity Incorporated and the Student Government Association (SGA). Throughout Jordan's time in SGA, he served as the Election Commissioner, Junior Class President, and Student Government Association President. Throughout his time as an undergraduate member of Omega Psi Phi, he helped lead Gamma Gamma Chapter to becoming the 9th District Social Action Chapter of the Year for their involvement in community activities and development.

Jordan graduated from Grambling in 2014 and went on to become a consultant with Accenture Federal Services in Harrisburg, PA. Following full time employment, Jordan and his family established the Harvey-Wilder Scholarship Foundation to encourage the next generation to attend HBCUs and to continue the legacy of HBCU exposure his parents instilled in him. Established in 2015, the Harvey-Wilder Foundation (HWF) was initially created for the purpose of raising awareness of HBCUs to high school seniors in Middle, GA. As HWF's reach expanded across the country, so too did its purpose. Today, in addition to multiple $1,000 scholarships awarded each year, the HWF provides mentorship and career support to its recipients. Throughout his professional career, he has worked closely with the government agencies including but not limited to the Department of Defense and the National Aeronautics and Space Administration (NASA) being a champion of HBCUs. In his free time, Jordan advocates for people of color in the beer industry in the mid-Atlantic and enjoys traveling. He currently resides in Silver Spring, Maryland, a suburb of Washington, D.C.

ADRAIN (AD) BONNER

Family...The Grambling Experience
Adrain (AD) Bonner

Historically Black Colleges and Universities have contributed greatly to American society and the world. Grambling State University (GSU) has a long-lasting tradition with many superstar name ambassadors as alumni and former students including Hall of Fame Coach Eddie Robinson, Super Bowl MVP Doug Williams, as well as entertainers such as Erykah Badu, E 40 and more. Grambling's long history is nostalgic and very prestigious.

The Grambling experience is family. The moniker GramFam is used amongst alumni and students to recognize the unique bond that is GSU. Long lineage of alumni families, traditions and customs passed down through generations, and historical significance to the culture of HBCU makes Grambling a standout. The geographic location of the university in the hills of a small city in north Louisiana transforms this little country town more of a big light, big city feel during football season and GSU Homecoming in particular.

The impact that Grambling State University has had on my life and career is immeasurable. Invaluable experiences and numerous relationships are at the top of my memories from GSU. As an incoming freshman, I anticipated meaningful moments but never did I imagine I would gain knowledge and build skills that are the foundation of my career. The experience I gained at GSU can never be measured

My first year at GSU and being a member in the World Famed Tiger Marching Band, I quickly learned the traditions and customs. The GSU band traveled to New York, Detroit, Dallas, and more within the first four football games of the season. The experience of flying as a large group, the 5-star hotels and meals, and playing at large professional sports venues were just a few highlights of my first season. Being such a stadium fanatic, marching on the fields of the Detroit Lions, The New York Giants, and my Dallas Cowboys were all remarkable opportunities for me personally. The first Bayou Classic I attended was such a breathtaking experience and never before had I seen anything like that atmosphere. It gave me motivation to be a better student and bandsman. The ambiance and culture of Bayou Classic played a huge factor in me wanting to continue to pursue music education and become a band director. I became a member of Kappa Kappa Psi National Honorary Band Fraternity in pursuit of band excellence.

As a sophomore I became Drum Major during the Cotton Bowl State Fair Classic vs Prairie View A&M University. Being in my hometown and supported by family and friends meant the world to me. After performing as GSU Drum Major for the first time my appreciation and determination skyrocketed. The try out process was very tiresome and grueling, but it taught me to endure and push through tough times. This experience will serve as a key component to the work ethic in my future.

My junior year I became Head Drum Major. During my tenure as head DM, GSU's band received numerous invitations to some of the greatest events in the country. Super Bowl XXXII halftime performance, President Bill Clinton Performance, Fox Sports Southwest and Cartoon Network commercials are just a sample of the experiences gained. Performing at the Super Bowl was a phenomenal experience along with artists such as Queen Latifah, Smokey Robinson, and Boys to Men. Learning the facilitation of corporate administration, production team, and artists working in unison was priceless. Grambling's band got to take a long-extended break simply because we were super ready. I always say that it was this Super Bowl performance that spearheaded the demand for exciting entertainment in the years to come. Super Bowl halftimes changed after that historical show.

My last two years at Grambling really catapulted my future. Composing for the band, choreographing steps, and coming up with ideas played a major factor in my future success. I had the opportunity to explore opportunities and responsibilities as a director from the student aspect. The communication with staff and also being the filter between them and students helped me learn and understand the value of customer service and teamwork. During my last year as Drum Major, I composed the infamous song Talking Out the Side of Your Neck. Although it had been played before by several bands, it was the arrangement that I wrote for Grambling that took over the world. Because of this enthusiastic rendition, all bands including predominantly white institutions play the song non-stop today. It proves that the culture of HBCU band music impacts everyone. At the end of my campus days I became a member of Omega Psi Phi Fraternity, Incorporated. Once I became an Omega Man, I understood the totality of my Grambling experience. Through fraternal life bonds of a lifetime were made. Invaluable experiences.

As a music education major, I was able to get the best of both departments. Grambling's long tradition of excellent professors was changing guard during my time there. I was glad to learn from some of the most outstanding educators who taught the concept of lifelong learners. That growth mindset has stayed with me through my career. As I reflect on the awesome staff in the education department, many of the projects and assignments are effective in today's current trends. For example, the usage of charts and diagrams that display concepts such as Bloom's taxonomy and more.

I am proud to be an alumnus of GSU. I serve on the staff for High School Band Camp as marching band director. In addition, I work many college recruiting fairs and help students from the Dallas Fort Worth area obtain admission and scholarships to GSU. I am passionate about students going on to college after high school. After taking numerous students to camps, I have helped over 75 students receive band scholarships to GSU. Many of those students have graduated and some are band directors currently. The GSU cycle of success continues to lead and represent all HBCU.

Being on the campus of an HBCU with a rich tradition as GSU is still beneficial to me today. No matter where I may go, when the G is represented outwardly, many alumni, current students, and supporters will recognize its uniqueness. I joke to many of my friends and even rivals that the G stands for Greatness State. I believe this wholeheartedly when one can visit anywhere and respect is given to Grambling, it makes me and all GSU alumni proud to be a part of the legacy.

About Adrain (AD) Bonner

Adrain Devine (AD) Bonner is an educational professional, band enthusiast, and advocator for HBCU.

AD, a native of Dallas, Texas, earned a bachelor's degree in Instrumental Music Education from Grambling State University (GSU). While AD was a student at GSU, he played the saxophone freshmen year and became drum major his sophomore year, serving 4 consecutive years for "The World Famed Tiger Marching Band".

AD received a master's in Music Education from The University of Texas at Arlington and a master's in Education Administration from The University of North Texas. He currently serves as Director of Music Education in Lancaster, TX.

In 1999, as head drum major, AD arranged the infamous song 'Talking Out the Side of Your Neck'. Over time The Grambling version written by AD became the staple that changed HBCU and bands all across the world. During AD's tenure as drum major, performances at Super Bowl XXXII, Cartoon Network Commercial, and meeting President Bill Clinton highlight a few of the many experiences he gained at GSU. AD has served GSU's High School Band Camp for several years working as assistant camp director, marching band director, and recruiting. In over 20 years of working in education, AD has helped send multiple students to and receive scholarships from bands at various HBCUs and all levels. AD received multiple awards including Rookie Teacher of the Year in 2001, Teacher of the Year in 2003, 2013, and 2019.

AD created his own entertainment company called Adeebo Productions. AD also performs as a saxophonist/ DJ entertainer by the stage name Saxxy Slim. In addition, AD hosts a podcast show interviewing various musicians from all HBCU and highlighting multiple aspects of HBCU experience. Thru collaborations, sponsorships, and partnerships AD hosts the largest high school Battle of the Bands in Lancaster, TX. This event helps kickoff the annual State Fair Classic Cotton Bowl Game between HBCU institutions Grambling and Prairie View in Dallas, Texas.

AD is a member of Omega Psi Phi Fraternity Inc., and Kappa Kappa Psi National Honorary Band Fraternity.

D. SCOTT

The Man, The Myth, The Legend!!!
D. Scott

Growing up in Texas, it is almost expected for high school seniors to pledge their allegiance to the University of Texas at Austin. It's one of the largest universities, in terms of enrollment, in the United States, and the school offers a wealth of academic programs that cater to anyone's career interests. But having grown up in Houston, Texas – the fourth largest city in the country –I knew that I needed something different from my environment. I needed a small, nurturing community, a community made up of people who looked like me. Grambling State University served as that place for me, and caused such a lasting impact on my overall development.

Grambling – located in the piney hills of north Louisiana – has no major department stores, one or two mom and pop eateries, and a post office. That is it. Students from large cities, like me, may frown upon the lack of amenities, but I quickly began to appreciate it. Because of the limited distractions, campus life played an integral role in my college experience. I learned everyone in my dorm and gained friends from encounters in the cafeteria, classes, and just meandering on "The Yard" – an HBCU term that just means the outdoor space where students gather and hang out. I became friends with folks who hail from the rural parts of the Deep South (their accents prove it), the palm trees found in Southern California, the bright lights of Las Vegas, and all places in between. This network I had joined expanded my horizons in a way that I do not believe would have occurred had I gone to a school in a major city.

Being involved in campus life taught me the importance of service. As the vice-president of the Student Union Board, I served as a voice for students to help plan the activities for the school year.

I listened to my peers, and I asked them what concerts and special guests they wanted to come onto campus. Planning a fun-filled homecoming week was a blast, as we welcomed comedians and artists onto campus. I served as President of the National Association of Black's in Criminal Justice. I also joined Kappa Alpha Psi Fraternity, Incorporated. This was another avenue for me to serve my peers and the Grambling community to organize events, such as clean-ups, listening sessions, voter registration drives, and other noteworthy occasions that would contribute to uplifting my people. To the brothers I never thought I needed, thank you Dr. Alexander Lodge, Bryant Brown, Chad Patterson, Justin Gay, Ashley Smith, Alan Mason, Brandon Gultery, Michael Terrell, Winston Sims, Brandon Joyner & Aubrey Jackson. As an adult, I know that it is my responsibility to still serve my neighbors in a capacity that will make our community a much better place.

Finally, going to my HBCU allowed me to become in-tune with my culture. As we all know, the American K-12 curriculum provides little to no insight on contributions made by Black people. We hear about Dr. Martin Luther King Jr. and Rosa Parks, and that is just about it. At Grambling, I was immersed in the true black experience. In my English classes, we focused on Black writers like Maya Angelou and Langston Hughes. We learned the Black National Anthem, "Lift Every Voice and Sing," and we sang it at convocations. Black intellectuals like Nikki Giovanni and Cornel West visited our campus and spoke with students and the community at large about the plight of Black Americans and how to navigate those challenges. And, of course, I would be remiss if I neglected to mention the outstanding alumni who answered the call and chose to return to the university to mentor and to encourage us while I was in school. Those moments shaped me into the man that I am today. I left the university knowing more about myself, my people, and the responsibility that I have to make my ancestors proud by living this life giving my all-in whatever career I choose.

After graduating from Grambling State University, I returned to Houston, my beloved home, and noticed more than a few places were different. I was different, too. I was not the same person as when I left as a soon-to-be 18-year-old, leaving my environment for a new one that was unfamiliar to me. Having a degree from Grambling State University has empowered me to   be a confident man who is a go-getter. I received the tools to navigate society. Those were the best four years of my life. The way I developed over those years would not have occurred in that fashion had I gone anywhere else. The structure, the people, the experiences – no offense – are just not anywhere but Grambling. I did not just choose Grambling State University. Grambling State University chose me, shaped me, and made me the person that I am today.

I was a teacher at Olle Middle School in Alief I.S.D. for over ten years while also being a very influential socialite and nightlife extraordinaire for over fifteen years. I am part of one of the biggest & most successful promotion teams that has the hottest events, venues, celebrity hosts, happy hours, restaurants, and much more in the Houston night light scene to this date. Live House Media continues to lead the pack by providing an unforgettable experience week in and week out. I am the co-founder of The Joey P and Scottie D. Foundation, The HSP Skills Camp is designed to teach young athletes about basic principles, and to incorporate these lessons while playing sports. "Have HEART. Be SMART. Take PRIDE." These three ideals are centered on providing motivation to the youth through knowledge of skills, to increase self-esteem and inspire kids to want to be successful on and off their field of play. I have a vending machine company entitled Snack's R Us and a transportation company, D.S. National Logistics, LLC. My daughter, Demi Adison Scott is the sole reason I strive for greatness each and every day because she's always watching. As parents, normally our goal is to provide a better lifestyle than we had growing up, give our children more opportunities and give beyond the necessities. Her mother and I wanted to take a different route to setting our daughter up for the future by launching her own doll and accessory line that highlights our true essence. It's Demi's World; we're just living in it.

Overall, I am here to inspire before I expire!!!

About D. Scott

D. Scott is a father, entrepreneur, former educator, criminal justice major, Kappa man, brother to an amazing sister, Danielle and God-fearing man. Born and raised in Alief, the southwest side of Houston, TX to the best parents a kid could have, Shirlene & Richard. Scott was heavily involved at church, academics and school sports as an adolescent. The various tools and talents that molded his success today were learned during those critical years. Upon graduating from Alief Elsik High School with honors while playing football and baseball, D. Scott knew he wanted to further his education at a Historically Black University. Grambling State University accepted that tall, slim, city boy with open arms & the rest is history.

STEVEN BALTAZAR AKA BZAR

"Grambling Dayz"
Steven Baltazar AKA BZAR

Picture riding in your car down the hill coming into the entrance of the campus. Seeing parents and students walking with suitcases, duffel bags, crates and most of all a spirit of Grambling in the air. The excitement building as you travel to your dorm to pick up your keys. The faces you pass that will one day become familiar acquaintances and others potentially lifelong friends. The experience of the first move in day as a Freshman on Grambling's campus is like no other day, it is the beginning of a new chapter and a see you later to what you experienced prior to getting to that small bowl of a city and school.

It was black love in the air, the same love my parents experienced as Gramblingnites in the 90's and me a baby tiger, attending Grambling nursery all those years ago and returning as a young adult to pave my future as a Grambling athlete and scholar. The first week of school I met one of my new teammates walking to practice, he was the first person I gave my phone number to. That relationship flourished into a rich and wealthy brotherhood that has lasted and strengthened over the years, along with a few more tried and true brothers placed in what we call the "Winnerz Circle". Major note to remember "Everyone you meet is not meant to stay, and every person that stays may not be meant to last." Be selective and selfish in your demands regarding loyalty and respect. You owe you the best in every situation, never downplay your worth.

I came to Grambling on a track scholarship, being a member of the Grambling Track team during a dominant era, was irreplaceable. We won four championships consecutively and in 2011 ranked 12th in the nation for our 4X1 relay team which we qualified for the

NCAA D1 national championships in Des Moines, Iowa at Drake Stadium. I was the 1st leg of that relay team setting a personal best in all of my races that year, the 100, 200 and 4x1 relay. Although we were by far the most winning team during my four year tenure at Grambling State University resulting in four SWAC CHAMPIONSHIP rings and an ALL AMERICAN D1 ATHLETE TITLE for five of us on that team in 2011, we didn't get the same respect or resources as the other team sports and yet we still prevailed. We were hungry for greatness and hard working independently and collectively. We moved as a brotherhood and our bond secured our success on and off the track. Real tigers in the jungle making major tracks.

In the spring of 2011, I crossed the burning sands of ALPHA PHI ALPHA, Delta Sigma Chapter. Being an Alpha man was instilled in me from birth. My father was an Alpha man, not the fraternal aspect but the exemplary definition of what an Alpha man is. Everything from the way he is respected to the way he gives without expectation, charitable, timely and monetary, to his ability to manifest things into reality from a positive vision, he is an Alpha man. From the way an Alpha man is supposed to respect and protect our black queens to having to acknowledge wrong in one's self and the flexibility to collaborate with other Kings for the greater good, without the aspect of jealousy or crab in a barrel mentality is what my father instilled in me. I joined a section of the divine 9 with hopes to further a journey of life enrichment, amongst like-minded individuals. In the years that have passed and the future that is to come I have learned that being an ALPHA MAN, has nothing to do with any fraternity. It is a lifestyle and duty of the very few righteous men and true warriors that are here on this earth, to make a portion or to enlighten a person to become the best versions of themselves through action, tested, tried and true. Remaining lifted and headed to the light, The ALPHA MAN is a mindset and state of being. It is much more than strolling and chanting. Not all that have crossed the sands of the fraternal aspect have been able to harness the fire and responsibilities that follow.

Attending Grambling I met the love of my life, going to my first Bayou Classic. I remember it every day, the first time I saw her. Blonde hair, slim, fine, white shirt with flowers, blue jeans, a walk of confidence and composure, graceful but bold, the face of a goddess, her spirit was radiant. Everyone's dream girl, the enchanting rivalry Southern Universities "The Dancing Dolls" Team Captain. The crowd stopped as she walked up the stairs of the JW Marriot going into the party that was held there, and she walked right past me completely unfazed. She was respected by men and women, she was a vision and humble, she moved the energy of the room with her presence, she is powerful. I was stuck, I had nothing to say but I knew she was my wife. A few years later, after hit and miss messaging and conversations we flourished into a team and created more life building a family. Even after the few years of no contact in between our college years until I graduated it made no difference. The seed was planted and rooted deeply from our first introduction, which paved the way for a healthy growing of our family tree. I am forever grateful for our journey, me the tiger and her the graceful jaguar we paired off perfectly. If I had not gone to Grambling it is possible, I might not have met my life partner, although I do believe I would have regardless. Grambling sped up that process and I am appreciative of our love story.

I have many memories of my tenure at The Grambling State University. Mostly involving in the best moments of each day with my friends and the pride of attending an HBCU. Being a Grambling athlete, pledging a fraternity, gaining brothers, and marrying my wife, it's immense love! Meeting people that didn't attend an HBCU is always interesting to hear how much of a different experience they had at their school. There is a special light that shines when you tell people you attended Grambling State University even if the band and Eddie Robinson is the first comment of reference. It shows the power and abundance of amazing opportunity and success from African American scholars, athletes, and creators over the span of numerous years. You appreciate the struggles and triumphs much more, understanding your role in the bigger picture, and that slogan "Where everybody is somebody" has real meaning and purpose to those that take the challenge. I love dear ole Grambling. Live Full.

About Steven Baltazar AKA BZAR

Mixed media contemporary artist who lives and works in Houston, Texas. He is the owner of BZAR STUDIOZ LTD. CO a design and illustration company. His distinctive personal styles emanates, surreality, peace and favor. BZAR express the vibrant spirit, colors, ideas and atmosphere of positivity with self-sustained winning through his artwork.

Graduating from Grambling state university with a bachelor's degree in criminal justice in 2012. He started his professional career as a police officer with the Houston Police Dept. working patrol in 3rd ward Houston for 4 years before promoting to Detective and spent his time serving in the Special Victims Unit for the next 6 years. He retired from the police department after 10 years of service, to follow his vision and began his favored career of being a professional artists and certified art teacher.

Bzar has done collaborative work with the Houston Police Dept, Universal Pictures, Comcasts, Fox network and many other notable businesses in the commercial industry. Looking to further his aspirations and vision to spread awareness to the masses on being true to self and free creativity promoting his tag line #liveFULL.

DR. KE'SHAWN ROBERTS AND KE'SHONE ROBERTS

Inseparable: A Bond That Can't Be Broken
Dr. Ke'Shawn Roberts and Ke'Shone Roberts

Imagine being accepted into a university that you were never accepted into. Sounds crazy, doesn't it? We arrived at Grambling State University in the spring of 2008 from New Orleans, Louisiana; we were ready to start our freshman year, or so we thought. Thank God we arrived early because I, Ke'Shawn, was accepted and enrolled while my twin sister, Ke'Shone, wasn't even in the system. The university was only tracking one of us the entire time. The staff in the registration office tossed out all of my sister's enrollment documentation thinking they had mistakenly received duplicate information. It was a silly mistake, but the University quickly fixed the error and enrolled Ke'Shone. However, there was a catch; Ke'Shone and I couldn't room together because I had a room assignment, and she did not. It wasn't the news we wanted to hear because we'd, practically, been conjoined at the hip since birth. Little did we know this was just the beginning to the life changing experience that is Grambling State University.

There is an Ancient Chinese Proverb that says, "An invisible thread connects those who are destined to meet, regardless of time, place, and circumstance. The thread may stretch or tangle. But it will never break." This was proven true for Ke'Shawn and I from the moment we settled into our separate dorms to now. It was a huge adjustment to no longer share your space with the one person who knew you best. It was important for us to find comfort in one of the most uncomfortable situations so we could receive all we went off to college for. It simply made no sense for us to shut down and be all in our feelings over our separation. We did drive our roommates crazy because we literally visited one another every day and talked on the phone every chance we got. Whew, and some of those visits and conversations weren't always pleasant. The more we stayed away from one another, the more intense they got. We are clearly known to be very loud and passionate about EVERYTHING. It was low-key entertaining too because our NOLA accents get heavy. Everyone was openly intrigued on how we talked let alone how we argued. It was comical, for them, to hear all that broken English. Anyway, there was simply nothing we could do about this new lifestyle Grambling State University had placed in our hands, and, despite the fact that Ke'Shone and I found ourselves in two different locations, the distance started to become somewhat normal.

Reality finally set in, and we were just fine. Mama said it all the time after a trillion calls to complain, "get over it, y'all are young adults now. Y'all ain't gonna die," in her most Cajun accent ever. There were several instances that we'd meet on the yard and be completely dressed alike from head to toe without having any conversation about wardrobe whatsoever. We even showed up to stalk and create a plan of how we will walk onto Grambling State's cheerleading squad by any means necessary. I remember vividly having rough times and needing Ke'Shawn. I would find that uncomfortable spot in my window to call her, because T-Mobile service sucked at that time, just to discover the phone ringing before I could even dial out. It would be her on the other end asking what was happening now. I knew I struck a nerve when she would call me by my middle name. We were each other's best friends, and we could feel when things were off. That freaky twin thing everyone accuses twins of is real.

After surviving our freshman year, we were able to be roommates our sophomore year. Sophomore year was interesting. We both applied for membership intake into Delta Sigma Theta, Sorority Incorporated. Unknowingly, we were both selected for interviews; however, we were made to believe only one of us was selected. This was to teach us a lesson in discretion on a new level. We both, secretly, got dressed and prepared for the scheduled interviews. We walked out of our rooms simultaneously to head to the interview location, but we soon saw each other heading in the same direction both dressed for an interview. If looks could kill, we would have both dropped dead in that moment. We both felt betrayed and bamboozled, but we were also full of joy and relief; we quickly chatted and wished each other good luck and positive vibes. A few days later, we were both selected for membership, and, after the process, we became sisters again; however, this time, we were sharing this bond with 46 other young women. Membership into the Sorority was another significant change for us. We found our own set of friends, got into relationships, discovered different interests, and were slowly becoming our own individuals. Sophomore year had finally ended. I joined ROTC and was sent off to Leadership Training Camp in Fort Knox, Kentucky for 4 weeks. Ke'Shawn stayed back and did summer school.

During my time at Leadership Training Camp, I had no means of communication aside from written communication, and I didn't have much time to do that because of all of the training. We realized this was the first, and longest, time we were physically separated. I missed my sister while she was in training, but I must admit I had some opportunities of self-discovery. I changed my major, which we shared, from Business Management to Kinesiology. That summer, I was able to do what I needed to do so we could still graduate together and on time. I knew Ke'Shone would freak out if we didn't graduate together. After my 4 weeks were up, we were finally reunited and caught up on all the missed time. I broke the news to Ke'Shawn that I had to now stay in ROTC allotted housing; therefore, we couldn't be roommates. However, it wasn't bad news anymore. What was once abnormal, and the worst news ever, became a new, well-adjusted lifestyle change for us. She moved off campus with one of her friends in an instant. I knew, good and well, that was her plan all along, tryna be slick. We were separated again, and, this time, it was consensual. Between living off campus and changing my major, we didn't see each other as much because I gave up JTS for the

Assembly Center. On the flip side, the ROTC building became my new home. It wasn't too bad because we still were teammates, we practiced and cheered at games together, participated in programs and community service with our Sorority, and found plenty of time to bond and socialize without completely neglecting one another.

Junior year was the hardest year for me; juggling school (which I was never the best at) ROTC, the Sorority, Cheer, and a host of other things had me feeling a burn-out. Ke'Shawn, on the other hand, was thriving! Getting inducted into honors societies, becoming a captain of the cheerleading squad, securing a dope internship, and, overall, just being the best example ever to me. Oh, yeah, she is the big sister by default because of those two minutes. Don't judge me, but it was time to use one of my lifelines. Perhaps we can finally reveal some of our secrets. I majored in business management while Ke'Shawn was a kinesiology major. If you're thinking, "no they didn't," YES, WE DID! We looked exactly alike, people could hardly tell us apart. So, yes, on Ke'Shone's worst days, I would go sit in her classes and get all that she needed. In return I'd eat on *her* meal plan, but she would go eat right behind me and tell Mrs. Miles, "oh, that wasn't me; that was my twin sister." Everyone knew Mrs. Miles wasn't sending you away from a meal; she was everyone's favorite. On days I couldn't get to campus, she would do the same for me. Ke'Shone tried asking me to take her PT test for her because she absolutely hated to run, but that was something I politely declined; I didn't care how many names she called me because of it. She assured me that no one would ever know, and no secret military agency was spying on us; however, I just couldn't bring myself to do it. Ke'Shone was so mad at that; she has always had a hard time adjusting to the word "no." I agreed to run *with* her but never *for* her. That compromise was very much appreciated while it lasted. One day, at cheer practice, I came down out of a stunt badly and tore my ACL. Ke'Shone quickly stepped in and found the time to help me through this injury. During the rest of that year Ke'Shone gathered all my schoolwork, brought me food, and was on call when I needed her.

She was my biggest cheerleader, she rooted me on during intense physical therapy and a full, speedy recovery. After that set back, I was as good as new with my newest accessory, a BIG, RED knee brace. Our junior year was coming to an end, and we were preparing for summer. I went on to lead the squad at NCA Cheer camp and completed part of my internship in Florida while Ke'Shone was sent off again to the Leadership Development Advancement Course in Fort Lewis, Washington. This time, she was allotted a little time to talk to family via base phone. We were now preparing for our last year at Grambling State University.

Senior year was a breeze, and we were just about accustomed to being separated. The final and best year flew by. We cheered side by side to the SWAC Championships, stepped, strolled, served on campus, and stayed on top of our studies. We competed that spring, one last time, together on the Bandshell and placed within the top four in the Nation. We graduated in May of 2012 at the top of our classes. Ke'Shone commissioned as an officer in the U.S. Army. At that moment, I knew the separation was concrete. I moved to Florida to attend the University of Miami to complete my Masters, work, and live my best life on Miami Beach while Ke'Shone was training in Fort Lee, VA. She then received a follow-on assignment to Fort Hood, TX. With the permanent distance between us, every conversation, and every visit, was cherished and enjoyed to the fullest. Her being on a battlefield in a full-on firefight lived in my head rent-free. The thought of getting that call, or receiving that flag, haunted me. However, I was a bit over dramatic to think her life was like the movies. She was stateside working, training, getting flown out, and always talking about these battle buddies. I made it my business to humble her every time by saying, "I'm yo only buddy, baby." After what felt like 20 years, Ke'Shone got medically discharged, and I received a call that would change EVERYTHING moving forward. She was now a free woman with tons of resources. We were both in a position where we could finally start something we dreamed of as little girls. I remember it like yesterday. I purchased that good, old, Spirit, one-way flight for the lowest price, and, best believe, I used my duffle bag as my personal item for free and headed to Killeen, Texas. Rising Stars 3lite Cheer, Dance and Tumbling was born. We were separated for a long time, and our shared passion reunited us. Ke'Shawn and I became roommates again after not living together for over six years. I'm not sure what was hardest for us, getting used to being in each other's space again or Ke'Shone transitioning into the civilian world. If "emotional roller coaster" had a meme, it would be us. We have Grambling State University to thank for discovering that sometimes it takes being apart for the better things to fall together. One separate room assignment was the life change we needed to help us discover who we were individually.

Life continues to go and grow. Ke'Shone established herself as a chef and the owner of D.I.ne "N" Owt Eatz. I am now Dr. Ke'Shawn Roberts. I own Dr. Correct Kinection, and B Thr3e LLC. This journey has been worth all the good, bad, and ugly. We both have beautiful daughters, and they have the same bond. However, we know Grambling State University is in their DNA on both ends, our LEGACY kids, heavy emphasis on the "G." They too may end up in that place where everybody is somebody to discover who they are.

About Dr. Ke'Shawn Roberts and Ke'Shone Roberts

Dr. Ke'Shawn Roberts and Ke'Shone Roberts are born and raised in New Orleans Louisiana and proud graduates of Grambling State University! The Roberts sisters were very active on campus! Grambling State Nationally Cheerleaders, members of Delta Sigma Theta Sorority, Incorporated. Delta Iota Chapter, FSUB, and Grambling State University Tiger Battalion ROTC program where one sister commissioned as an active-duty Logistics Officer. The popular duo did so much more. With over 20 years of cheer and dance experience these girls along with their oldest sister began to live out a lifelong dream of theirs! They are co-owners of Rising Stars 3lite Cheer, Dance and Tumbling in Central Texas with two new expansion locations loading! Together they are a force and separately soaring beyond measures! Dr. Ke'shawn is the owner of Dr. CorRECt Kinection and B Thre3 LLC in which she specializes in Recreation Consultation, Sporting Event Planning, Sports Recruiting and all things Crafty. while Retired Veteran Ke'Shone is a rising Chef and owner of D.I.ne N Owt Eatz where she specializes elevated pastries, catering, meal preparation, all-natural baby food, the ultimate private chef experience and so much more. The twin sisters are mothers of two baby girls Blaise' Roberts (3) and the new edition Kei'Auni Johnson. This is only the start for the Roberts Sister as they continue to Rise, create generational wealth and reach new Goals Daily.

TERRANCE D. GILES JR.

Growing Up Grambling, A Continued Legacy
Terrance D. Giles Jr.

I grew up on Grambling's campus. No, seriously! I grew up on Grambling's campus. My mom was pregnant with me while she was in school at Grambling. Which means I was on the yard even before I was born! WOW! I have really gone from going to class with my mom while she was pursuing her degree in Institutional Food Production Management to pursuing my degree in Hotel and Restaurant Management, while my mom served as the Special Events Coordinator for the Hospitality Department. I went from going to the concerts and Greek shows with my parents to performing on stage for the Greek show with my mom there to support. I went from getting off the bus at the Property and Receiving Department where my dad was the Warehouse Supervisor to working right next door to my dad as the Supervisor in Tiger Express while he was the Director of the Mail Room. By the time I was enrolled as a student at Grambling I had already done everything there was to do in college, but I was a kid with his parents. The experience as a student was completely different!

I had no intentions of going to school. I started working my first "official" job exactly one week after I turned eighteen, April 14th, 2003, to be exact. I was a line cook at Sonic in Grambling. I started a second job that June as an Event Specialist at the Ruston Civic Center. I was just going to work, making money, and venturing into the world of entrepreneurship. My mom came home one day with a folder. As she handed it to me, I looked at her and said, "what's this?" She replied, "it's your class schedule." Being that she was working in the Hotel and Restaurant Management department she already had my classes set. My thoughts were Ma, I'm not going to school but knowing Gwen Giles if I would have said that I probably wouldn't be alive today to tell this story. So my thoughts remained just that, thoughts. However, I did not open the folder to look at the schedule. I just simply said, "okay' and put the folder on the desk next to the computer.

It is now August, and it is time for the dorms to open so the students can move in. I called a few friends to see if they were hitting the yard. Of course, they were! We knew the exact spots to post up at. The spots where everyone had to pass through. I was there for one reason and one reason only. I wanted to see the "guhs"' as my high school basketball coach would say. Yes! I went on the yard to see what new and returning young ladies were out there. After a few nights of seeing all the pretty ladies and they kept asking me what my major was I decided to go home and open the folder. I memorized my entire schedule so that I would be able to talk about it the next time someone asked. When classes started on that Monday, I was officially a student. Well, not actually official just yet. All my life I have heard the saying, "Grambling State University. The place where everybody is somebody." I honestly believed that! The city of Grambling is such a small community that everyone knows everyone. It was a beautiful thing! However, I found out quickly why "with a fee sheet" was added to the statement by students. Although my mom had my schedule set for me, I still had to complete the registration process. It took a while, but I got my fee sheet. Now that saying "Grambling State University. The place where everybody is somebody, with a fee sheet" started to make more sense now. You are indeed somebody at Grambling, but you better make sure you have that fee sheet. So, there I was going to class and enjoying it. The yard was always live. I was convinced that one day there would be a documentary about my life, so I always carried a camcorder with me to document everything that was going on. Especially when BET Black College Tour came to campus, Homecoming, Bayou Classic, and of course Spring Fest.

Things really got interesting my sophomore year when I started working in the café. I had one class on Tuesday and Thursday which was a late afternoon class, so I went to work early on those days. That 6 AM to 2 PM shift was tough, especially on Tuesday for pancake day. It seemed like all five thousand plus students that were enrolled in school at the time wanted pancakes. I later found out that it really was not the pancakes, it was the tall handsome guy with the pretty eyes that was cooking and serving the pancakes that had all the girls in the line. At the time I had no idea how significant it was for me to work in the cafeteria. It was one other student working there at the time. We were in the same department, and we were able to satisfy our intern hours right there on campus, get paid for working, and still take a couple extra classes if we chose to do so. I was able to not only serve the students in the cafe but also work with catering for all the different events on campus and even served in the press box during the home football games. That also led to me being offered to work with the business department for the Bayou Classic. Working, learning how things operate, and having fun! I was not passing up on that opportunity.

I started to get more involved with extracurricular activities on campus. I joined black Dynasty Modeling. I had an interest in modeling so I figured I would try it out. Plus, some of the prettiest women on campus were a part of Black Dynasty. We become family. The cookouts (I was on the grill of course), building lifelong relationships with good people, and learning modeling techniques that I can still do today were all beneficial experiences. I also participated in the Men of Essence Showcase hosted by the Society of Distinguished Black Women. I had no interest in it but my friend who was the co-chair for the event gave me the packet one day and told me I was going to do it. When I did not show up for the interest meeting, she called me and had some very colorful words for me. So, I went to the meeting and decided to do it just for fun. I became the inaugural Mr. Man of Essence in which I was on the cover and centerfold of a calendar.

In the Spring of 2005, the Kappa interest meeting flyers went up. My best friend at the time called me to see if I saw it. We have been talking about this since high school. I honestly was not going to go because we had an intramural basketball game that same night. He had to convince me to not come to the game and go to the meeting, so I went. It was a good thing that I decided to go through with the Men of Essence Showcase and join Black Dynasty because it all came into play for being chosen as a member of the Gamma Psi Chapter of Kappa Alpha Psi Fraternity, Inc. Even me being the Special Events Coordinator for the Hospitality Club played a key role. Once I became a member, I became the Hospitality Coordinator for the chapter. Any event that we hosted that needed food I coordinated it. My dad, who has owned his own catering business since I was four years old, provided the food for all our events. In Fall 2006 when we needed a couple extra people to join the step team, I decided to give it a go. Practice for the step team was like a part time job. Six a.m... campus runs to make sure we had the stamina on stage, and we still had two-a-day practices. I loved every minute of it. I sprained my ankle two weeks before the Bayou Classic Step Show but there was no way I was going to miss that. My ankle and foot were swollen and purple, but it did not matter not one bit. I still made every practice and performed on that stage in front of thousands of people. We got second place but the experience itself was amazing!

I could go on for days about The Grambling State University and all the good times and experiences I had there. Grambling State University is a major part of The City of Grambling, La. And it really is one big family. You come in not knowing much of anything or anyone, but you leave with a family. It truly is the place where everybody is somebody, just make sure that you have your fee sheet though!

About Terrance D. Giles Jr.

Terrance D. Giles Jr., also known as T.J., is currently working with Houston ISD as an At-Risk Program Administrator. He is also an Assistant Basketball Coach at Worthing High School. T.J. has more than ten years of coaching experience working with athletes from middle school through the collegiate level. Before moving to Houston T.J. spent 3 years as the Assistant Basketball Coach for Centenary Men's Basketball team. While there he coordinated the strength and conditioning program for the team and won the 2020 SCAC (Southern Collegiate Athletic Conference) Tournament Championship. T.J. is preparing to launch his company which is a conglomerate of services catered to coaches and athletes that focus on holistic development.

T.J. began his school daze in the fall of 2003 as a freshman at Grambling State University where he majored in Hotel and Restaurant Management. He was also a part of the Hospitality Club, serving as President, Vice President, and Special Event Coordinator. He was the Inaugural Man of Essence, a showcase to highlight the outstanding young men on campus, hosted by The Society of Distinguished Black Women. T.J. was also initiated into the Gamma Psi chapter of Kappa Alpha Psi Fraternity, Inc. during the spring semester of 2005 and was a part of the Gamma Psi Step Team. T.J. attended culinary school at Orlando Culinary Academy from 2007 to early 2009. He then returned to Grambling to complete his last year of undergraduate studies and received his bachelor's degree in May of 2010.

KRISTY LASHAUN BURRELL

Cheers to My Grambling Experience
Kristy Lashaun Burrell

My name is Kristy Lashaun Burrell and here's my story. Growing up in Algiers, of New Orleans it has always been different obstacles for young adults who have the potential to succeed after high school. Other than people working front line careers symbolizing their successful transitions into adulthood, there wasn't many role models for my leisure due to lack of exposure. As a high school student I had the opportunity to be a part of the cheer, track, and flag team. Being exposed to these activities helped develop the skills which paved the way in my black college experience. I can thank my community who never allowed me to forget my mother's legacy as a track star and what she meant to them. I'm forever grateful for the inspirational words from Coach Lewis and others who motivated me to think further than what was in front of me.

I worked hard and received six track and field scholarships to several Historic Black Universities which I sadly missed out on. Initially, I didn't have a desire to attend college until a life altering incident occurred with my friends. This uncharacteristic event was a vital eulogy for me in recognizing the need to better myself. Still uncertain of what I wanted to do, that experience showed me the life I did not want for myself. After that I asked my mother if it was too late to go to college. She told me it was never too late to do anything. My mother rented a car the next day and we were headed to Grambling State University.

Five hours away from my hometown, my mom and I made it to Grambling, Louisiana which turned out to be my home for the next five years. My freshman year was full of emotions, opportunities, and decisions that needed to be made. That year I became the first person in my immediate family to go to college. Being away exposed me to what it felt like to be alone, away from family and friends. Leaving everything behind with the purpose of bettering oneself. Allowing myself to go in the direction of fear has been one of the greatest decisions I've made.

During the second semester of my Freshman year, I encountered a guy named Terry Lilly at the bookstore. Terry Lilly introduced himself as the cheerleading coach. After a brief discussion telling him I was there to run track he suggested I try out for the cheer team. Even though I was scared, I showed up for the 2004-2005 cheerleading tryouts ready to do the unthinkable. I felt all emotions but pride and determination forced me to give it my all even though I was shy and timid. I was able to perform up to standard and secured a spot on the GSU cheer team. After my first year of college, I went home for the summer to see my family. I loved everything about being in New Orleans, but I felt the desire to want more. As my summer was ending, I headed back to GSU for "Cheer Hell Week" and to move into my new off campus apartment. I had no idea that everything I knew about home would change forever.

In August 2005, hurricane Katrina hit New Orleans in a devastating way. I was truly thankful that I had moved off campus as I was able to house my dislocated family during a time of crisis. That was such an uncertain time for everyone affected. I was slightly disconnected from school because of the life lessons. Cheerleading was the highlight of that year as it allowed me to be a part of something and kept me motivated. I was able to see the world through different aspects of life. Being a part of GSU Cheer team taught me self-discipline, self-worth, and self-satisfaction. I went to practice daily, I worked hard at doing my part. Coach Lilly was superhuman to most, he played a valuable role in my life. As I can recall, he embodied his passions and goals which he turned into occupations. I have never witnessed someone achieve a successful career in that matter. I believe so much of my success in life happened because I imitated a good portion of Coach Lilly's behavior. All my father figures were providers who just worked to raise their families, but Coach Lilly was the first male figure who I've witnessed doing what he loved and created a way to get paid to live his everyday lifestyle. I had my first dosage of that level of success as a cheerleader. We received stipends while cheering at GSU. Though not much, my first experience earning money while doing what I love to do was a great money management lesson to learn. I strive to continue to hold my spot and make the travel squad, from 2004-2009 I was blessed to be cheerleader. My last year on the cheer team we placed fourth in the nation at the NCA national cheer competition.

One of the most flattering experiences while attending GSU was being a contestant in the Grambling State University Miss Cover Girl Pageant. That was one of the most feminists' things I have ever been a part of in my life! The theme of the pageant was Dream Girls. I enjoyed dressing up for all three categories and my favorite part was the opening act dance. I placed third in the calendar which earned me Miss October. I was inspired by the pageant and what it instilled in me as a young woman. Maybe one day I will organize a pageant to expose the young ladies of my community to the core values I have learned.

Grambling State University student experience was one for the books. How could I not mention the yard, the parties, the BET college experiences, spring fest and homecoming, Football season, Basketball season, and all the parties that fall in between. The yard was my personal favorite, it reminded me of the green box in my neighborhood back home where all the kids met up daily. The yard was the common meet up place for the entire student body. That's where all the Sorority and Fraternity plots were located. Unfortunately, when my time arrived sorority activities were suspended so I was not able to experience pledging and joining any other sisterhoods outside my cheer involvements. The yard was the hangout, a place where students would gather before and after class. Every day it was something new, from block parties to step shows, and fashion shows for others. The yard was a place to exchange ideas, I have made a lot of connections that to this day I have utilized in my network. There are many times I wish I could have done more and built more relationships with others, but time goes so fast when you are having fun. I did form some great relationships with people I will never forget.

I can recall cheering at the Eddie Roberson stadium, "the hole" in front of fans supporting their favorite HBCU teams. It was such a great experience, so many of us continue to go back each year for homecoming just to feel the rush. Grambling State University was a place where I made my transition from a teenager to a young strong black woman. I honestly believe I would not be who I am today if I hadn't had my Black college experience. As of today, those experiences have exposed me to various opportunities and have been some of my best happenings. Looking back, I am truly proud of myself and those decisions I made to get me where I am.

I graduated from Grambling State University with a Bachelor of Science in May 2009. I have been able to utilize my degree and accomplishments to further my life successes and goals. Currently, I am a High School teacher where I am also the head cheer coach. I operate my own business (Daily Life Managements LLC), which provides clients with the awareness and tools to create a process of change. The goal of Daily Life Managements is to help the youth and their families become better by focusing on necessary skills to help them with their everyday life obstacles.

I take pride in encouraging and supporting others with staying motivated and on task. My professional goals are to keep developing programs that are needed to help improve the community and build stronger family dynamics. One of my favorite quotes by Franklin D. Roosevelt is "There are many ways of going forward, but only one way of standing still." I plan on teaching everyone that crosses my path the lessons I have learned. I will also share my Black College experiences in hopes of motivating others to take chances to create a better life. In conclusion, I am forever grateful for my Black College experience. The Lessons I learned throughout this journey I would not trade for world. Dear Grambling State University teachers, coaches, and administrators, I Kristy Burrell would like to say thank you. Your work and dedication did not go unnoticed, I can truly agree with Grambling State University motto that GSU is the place where everybody is somebody.

About Kristy Lashaun Burrell

Ms. Kristy Lashaun Burrell is a New Orleans Native and a proud graduate of Grambling State University class of 2009. She earned a Bachelor of Science in Criminal Justice and was a part of the Grambling State University Cheerleading team. Ms. Burrell is currently a high school educator, cheer coach, and professional life coach who specializes in anger management and domestic violence. She is the founder/ owner of Daily Life Managements LLC, Manage Life Daily, and Timeless Pieces LLC. Ms. Burrell take pride in encouraging and supporting others with professional as well as personal issues. She has a passion for motivating others to stay on task, and believe that opportunities don't Just happen, they are created by how you live life on a daily.

Ms. Burrell has over 13 years of social service experiences within the criminal justice field working with youths and families on ways to managing anger, battling mental health issues, and overcoming social anxiety brought on from Trauma within the inner cities of New Orleans. She has conducted multiple parenting courses, linked individuals to long term services, and provided educational services to small and large groups on ways to display effective communication and appropriate behavior at home, school, and within the workplace. As an Educator teaching reading and business communication, Ms. Burrell not only work within regular school hours she is the high school cheerleading coach training young ladies to express their feelings, release their emotions, and show their creativity through cheer.

Ms. Burrell has conducted over three hundred hours of community service partnering with multiple mental health agencies, gate keepers, stakeholders, and community leaders to work with improving our school systems and bettering our communities. She will continue to be a mentor, social justice advocate, and teacher, working to change the negative spectrum on the city of New Orleans within the justice and school systems.

Ms. Burrell plans are to expand both her nonprofit and for-profit agencies throughout the entire state of Louisiana providing services through Justice and School systems to individuals in need. To obtain more information on services provide through Daily Life Managements check out the website at www.dailylifemanagements.com or you can follow us for additional information @MANAGELIFEDAILY on IG.

DONALD R. WILLIAMS, JR., ESQ.

EXIT 81

Donald R. Williams, Jr., Esq.

I remember my first days as an incoming freshman student at Grambling State University like it was yesterday. On Saturday, August 10th, 2002, my dad and I flew into Dallas-Fort Worth International Airport from Los Angeles International Airport. After collecting my entire room's worth of luggage from baggage claim, we headed toward the exit doors. There were two sets of double doors at the exit that led to outside. Once the second set of double doors opened, I was hit by a wall of thick, barely breathable air that caused my sunglasses to fog up and blur my vision; it almost caused me to have an asthma attack—something that I had not experienced since early childhood. This was my first time in "The South." Unlike some students, I had not visited Grambling State University prior to the beginning of my matriculation at the university. I had not experienced southern humidity prior to this day. Nonetheless, we picked up our Ford Escape rental car and began our four-hour drive down Interstate 20 to 403 Main St., Grambling, Louisiana 71245, which would become my place of residence for the next five years

Upon approaching the City of Grambling, I was extremely excited to see our exit sign "Exit 81, Louisiana Highway 149, Grambling," because I was both tired from the long drive and ready to see the university I had selected to attend. My face was plastered to the passenger window, viewing every person, place, and thing we passed while traveling down LA-149. We drove for about two or three minutes before coming to a stop at the first intersection with a traffic light. It seemed like we were stopped for a long time or maybe I was just nervous and anxious. I looked up and read the street sign "Martin Luther King Jr Ave," and noticed the street we were traveling down was called "RWE Jones Dr." I noticed a church sign that read "New

Rocky Valley Baptist Church," and I also noticed that the road we were traveling continued on to what appeared to be a bridge or a hill of which I could not see beyond.

The light turned green, and we proceeded to drive over the hill. When we reached the top of the hill, I saw academic buildings to the right and a "Grambling State University" sign on the left. My first thought was "I made it." My second thought was "Is this what the 'dirty south' looks like?" The "dirty south" was a phrase I heard in many rap song lyrics in reference to Bible Belt states like Louisiana. Anyhow, I was not sure what to think of this new and different environment. As I had grown up in the fast-paced, big city environment of Los Angeles, California, I was trying to wrap my head around the slow-paced, small-town vibe I was getting from Grambling, Louisiana.

The goal for the day was to arrive at Grambling State University and locate my dorm hall and room, so I focused on the goal. It wasn't yet move-in day, but I wanted to make sure that I knew exactly where to arrive when it was my time to move-in. I was assigned to Garner Hall. We entered Grambling's campus and headed to Garner Hall. When we arrived, I saw that it was different from most of the other dorm halls. The entrance to each dorm room was on the outside of the building and not the inside like the other men's dorm halls in the area—back in 2002, the men's dorms were on the east side of Main St. and the women's dorms were on the west side of Main St. Garner Hall was situated between Attucks Hall and the baseball field. My assigned room was the second door on the first floor facing the baseball field. After viewing Garner Hall, we headed to Walmart, as most incoming freshmen did, to purchase some necessities for my survival in my dorm room and being away from my parents.

The next day, Sunday, August 11th, 2002, was move-in day at Grambling State University. My dad and I arrived at Garner Hall early in the morning with everything we purchased at Walmart the previous day. I checked-in with Garner Hall's Resident Assistant to confirm my room assignment and receive my room key. After I received my key to Room 102, my dad and I unloaded the car and filled my dorm room.

The next couple of days kicked off Freshman Orientation Week at Grambling State University, and they were a blur as I completed the registration process for school: I stood in a long line in the Intramural Center to register for school; I sat in the Financial Aid Office (Lee Hall) for a few hours to solidify that my tuition was being paid; I retrieved the necessary proof of registration (i.e. "fee sheet") from the Cashier's window in the Administrative Building (Long-Jones Hall) because Grambling State University is "the place where everybody is somebody (with a fee sheet)"; lastly, I registered for classes.

As I reflect on the different key moments in my life, while at Grambling State University, I have come to realize that the immediate connections I made while registering for classes in the Earl Lester Cole's Honors College, located in Charles P. Adams Hall, began a domino effect of events that led to me having an exciting and enjoyable experience at Grambling State University. Up to that point, I had not really spoken to any students or established any connection with any of the students. When I entered the Earl Lester Cole's Honors College office, I was thrust into a small environment and was surrounded by several other students who were also registering for classes. We were all gathered around a conference room table with course catalogs, and one of the Earl Lester Cole Honors College counselors provided guidance to us all regarding our respective degree program interests.

While the process of choosing classes was slow and nerve-racking, as I naively felt my course selection was the end-all be-all determinant for the trajectory of the rest of my life, I began to meet other like-minded students in the room. "Like-minded" meaning we all felt the anxiety associated with choosing classes in our respective degree programs, and we were all there with similar goals, i.e., to graduate and to be a successful, contributing member of society. The students I met while in that conference room represented some of the best and brightest from all over the country. We began to connect with one another, some of us exchanged dorm hall locations and the last four digits of our dorm room phone numbers—because the first three numbers were the same for all students. Others made plans to meet up later that day or the next day. By the end of the orientation week, I found myself congregating on the steps of Jewett Hall (a women's dorm) in the evening with several incoming freshmen students, men and women, from various parts of the country. We spent many evenings together on the Jewett Hall steps thereafter. We talked, laughed, played, cried, and, most importantly, bonded. These were the people that made my adjustment to young adulthood bearable and fun. Many of us experienced similar culture shock and even homesickness—but we had each other. We were, in many ways, each other's support system. For me, not only was this the beginning of what would be life-long friendships, it was also the foundation of what would be my ever-growing web of connections and friendships, my Grambling network, or what I, and my fellow Gramblinites, affectionately call "GramFam."

Now, whenever I am traveling down Interstate 20 and heading toward the City of Grambling, the excitement I experience when I see "Exit 81, Louisiana Highway 149, Grambling," is no longer simply because I have made it to my destination. I get excited to see "Exit 81" because it means I am home.

About Donald R. Williams, Jr., Esq.

Donald R. Williams, Jr. grew up in Carson, California and graduated from San Pedro High School. Mr. Williams attended the historically black university, Grambling State University, in Grambling, Louisiana, where he earned a Bachelor of Arts degree in Paralegal Studies and a Bachelor of Arts degree in Criminal Justice.

After graduating from Grambling State University, Mr. Williams was employed as a litigation paralegal and, later, a litigation support specialist, in the Los Angeles office of Kirkland & Ellis LLP. When Mr. Williams' desire to become an attorney became too much to overcome, Mr. Williams moved to New Orleans, Louisiana and began law school at Tulane University Law School. Mr. Williams received his Juris Doctor from Tulane University Law School.

After law school, Mr. Williams was employed as an associate attorney at the Bohm Law Group, Inc. and, later, The Rosa Law Group. As an attorney at these firms, Mr. Williams received extensive legal training and engaged in competent legal representation from A to Z. Mr. Williams prosecuted hundreds of demanding private and public sector employment discrimination, wrongful termination, and wage and hour violation cases. From managing and supervising client intakes and consultations to research, negotiations, mediation, and trial and post-trial practice, Mr. Williams has developed the advocacy skills, knowledge, and experience to a degree that allows him to comfortably and confidently handle a broad range of legal issues.

Prior to opening up his own practice, Mr. Williams was employed as an associate attorney at Weintraub Tobin Chediak Coleman Grodin law corporation. Mr. Williams represented clients from a diverse range of industries, including professional sports, healthcare operations, agricultural and food processing industries, education institutions, restaurants, and the service industry. The work environment at Weintraub Tobin was fast-paced, demanding, and constantly changing, which made every day different, the legal questions Mr. Williams confronted complex, and has accustomed Mr. Williams to taking calculated business and legal risks when necessary.

As a Visiting Law Professor at University of California-Davis School of Law, Mr. Williams teaches electronic discovery and digital evidence to law students. Mr. Williams designed and developed a one-semester course, "Electronic Discovery and Digital Evidence", to provide students with the procedural and practical knowledge and skills needed to be successful in modern litigation.

In 2017, 2018, 2019, 2020, 2021, 2022, and 2023 Donald was named a recipient of The National Black Lawyers' "Top 40 Under 40" Award for the state of California. The award recognizes the nation's top lawyers under the age of 40 who exemplify a broad range of high achievement, including legal prowess, leadership, and community involvement. Additionally, Donald was selected to Super Lawyer's Northern California Rising Stars list in 2021, 2022, and 2023, an honor reserved for those lawyers who exhibit excellence in practice, and only 2.5% of attorneys in Northern California receive this distinction.

JOUELLE YOUNG

A Classic Experience
Jouelle Young

I never thought that I would go to college. It was never something that I had dreamed about doing. My mom gave me no options. She just told me that I needed to choose a college to go to, and I needed to choose fast. A week after high school graduation, I decided to go with Grambling State University.

I knew absolutely no one, but I decided to make the best out of my experience. One of the things that I decided to do was to become a dancer. I loved the movie Drumline and I loved watching the girls dance with the band. So once I got to Grambling, I said to myself, "How hard can this be?" Little did I know this was one of the hardest things I could have ever tried to do. To become a dancer at Grambling State University you must have a wide range of dancing techniques. Unfortunately, I had none. Also to become a dancer for Grambling State University, you had to try out for each game. It wasn't like other HBCU dance teams. We were a dance company and to dance with the band was a privilege and also a great accomplishment. Not only do you have to be in physical shape but you also have to execute every dance move perfectly. Since this was my freshman year, I became extremely discouraged. and I did not dance. Every game I would sit next to the band and the dancers wishing that it was me. Freshman year came to an end and I promised myself I would go back and dance even if I have to start at the bottom.

The time is now sophomore year and dance camp has begun. At dance camp I was trained by some of the greatest dancers, and they helped me with my confidence and technique. Ms. Diane Marone Grigsby was the director at the time, and she got me into shape. After about five games went by, she allowed me to audition to dance in the stands with the veteran dancers. I honestly did not know what she saw in me. I only asked to audition just to ask, I had no clue she would actually tell me yes. So I had my first audition in front of the Veteran dancers. This audition was extremely intimidating, but somehow I made it through, and somehow I made it to dance in the stands. This was the start to my dance career at Grambling State University. Once I got the hang of dancing in the stands, she began to allow me to audition for the field shows. Of course I didn't make any field shows because I couldn't even do a pirouette turn. So I worked my butt off to try to gain some technique. Sophomore year came to an end but the dancing didn't come to an end for me. I went home and took every dance class that I could so that when I got back for my junior semester, I would make the field.

Now here we are in junior year. This was the year that I had developed as a great dancer. I came back to the studio with confidence, and Ms. Maroney didn't have any more comments for me. See the thing about Ms. Morrone is that if she corrects you often it is definitely because you need it, but once she stops correcting you, it means you're doing something right. Not only did I come back as a great dancer ESPN decided they wanted to do a reality series on the band and the dancers called "The Battle". I was chosen as one of the main characters for the reality show. This is one of the greatest moments of my life, because not only was I featured on a reality hit series, but I also got to showcase my talents that I worked so hard to develop. This show followed our day-to-day campus activities and how we balanced attending an HBCU, while being dedicated to the band and dance team.

Football season is the best season at any HBCU. We had a game every Saturday. Some games were away and some games were home. The best games in my opinion were the home games because there was so much support. The entire university would come to the games as well as people who live in the city of Grambling. Now, although I did like the home games, I loved traveling. Every time we would travel, the people would literally treat us like royalty. We did not ride on regular school buses, or travel buses. We always traveled in style with an RV style bus. If we wanted to go to sleep, we would just hop in our bunk beds. The energy from any game, whether they be home or away, was the best energy I had ever experienced. The Bayou Classic by far was the best game for us to dance. We met so many celebrities, we danced for so many different occasions, and we experienced so much more than the normal 19, 20-year-old experienced in their lives. For the Bayou Classic, we would have to dance a good four times. There was battle of the bands, there was a bayou classic parade, there was the pregame, and then there was halftime. Dancing for bayou classic halftime was a very big honor, because not only were we performing for thousands of people, we were also performing on live television. There was no room for mistakes or errors. This was the time that you danced your heart out. I was blessed enough to dance three Bayou Classics and each time the experience got better and better.

If it wasn't for attending Grambling State University, I would not have experienced any of this. Grambling State University, and Miss Diane Maroney Grigsby made these opportunities possible for me. I will always have a special place in my heart for Grambling State University. If it worked for me, it can definitely work for you.

About Jouelle Young

Jouelle Young is thirty-two years old, a mother of one, and a full-time entrepreneur. She is The Owner of The J Slay Studios located in Dallas, Texas. She attended Grambling from 2008-2012 where she served as Ms. Gold for Alpha phi Alpha Fraternity Incorporated. She was Ms. Covergirl Runner up, a member of The Orchesis Dance company and a member of The Alpha Theta chapter of Alpha Kappa Alpha Sorority, Incorporated. Lastly, she was a cast member of the hit show "The Battle". The scripture she lives by is Phillipians 4:13.

WILLIE MILLER

Meeting Mrs. Maroney Grigsby and Starting My Career!

Willie Miller

My experiences at Grambling State University has been nothing short of greatness. Mr. Troy Poplous is who I'd like to thank for teaching me theater and acting at McDonogh 35 High School. Mr. Poplous started me on my way as an artist and still pushes me to continue my growth today. It is because of him, I attended Grambling State University to pursue my growth as an artist. I now have a plethora of stories and memories from Grambling State that I will always cherish. I have many memories at Grambling State University such as being a Theatre Major, Collegiate Cheerleader, Dance Minor, Orchesis Dance Company member, pledging Cheer Phi Leader, Phi Nu Pi Honor Society, and so many more. However, one of the most highlighted memories I will discuss is meeting Mrs. Dianne Maroney Grigsby, Grambling State University Orchesis Dance Company-Artistic Director. She is one of the many people who set me on a path to being a performing artist, teacher, choreographer, actor, and overall entertainer that I am today.

It was my freshman year as a Theatre Major, I was a cheerleader for Grambling State and also a part of the first play of the season, "The Wiz". I was cast for the character, Royal Gatekeeper, who guarded the gate leading into The Emerald City. Not only did I meet some of my lifelong friends during this production, but I was also introduced to Mrs. Maroney- Grigsby. She was the director of the Orchesis Dance Company and all things Dance within the Department of Performing and Visual Arts. She was the choreographer for "The Wiz" and the Orchesis were the featured dancers in the production. She was full of energy and elegance. She was the epitome of what a true artist is. We were eventually introduced, and she said, "You should join the dance company."

I've always wanted to dance because knowing the dance art form would work in correlation with me as an actor and make me more versatile artist. However, I never knew how to do so. Yet, little did I know meeting Mrs. Grigsby would change all that. Unlike most HBCU's, Grambling State University Orchesis Dance Company is not just a team of girls who dance with the band. The Orchesis Dance Company is run like a professional company where you have dance classes for formal training and partake in numerous performances including football games, basketball games, Grambling State Coronation, Dance His High Praise annual spring concert, and so much more. The company is also connected to the dance minor in which I was planning to enroll in. If you are in the dance minor program it is mandatory that you are in the company for the performance aspect of dance. I was on board after seeing the dancers and realizing that males can join the dance company. Even though I wasn't on board physically just yet, mentally I was prepared. I wanted to finish my season as a cheerleader and finish my pledging process for Cheer Phi Leader, a non-Greek cheer organization. I tried attending cheer and dance practices for one week. That was one of, if not, the most exhausting times of my college career trying to balance cheer, dance, being cast in productions, and school. I'm sure I seemed like a fickle kid that didn't know what he wanted to do. However, I've always been clear about my goals and aspirations. Finally in my second semester as a freshman, I fully committed to being a part of the Orchesis Dance Company. Soon after, I picked up a minor in dance.

I must say, meeting Mrs. Grigsby has made me the artist I am today. During our time together she graced my foundation as a dancer and made me her assistant. I assisted with dance classes, behind-the-scenes paperwork, and whatever else needed to make her duties flow seamless and smoothly. It is quite an honor to say that I was the assistant and formally trained by a former Alvin Ailey Dance Theatre member. Alvin Ailey Dance Theatre is one of the most prestigious modern dance companies in the world located in New York, New

York. She took me everywhere with her from dance camps, workshops, and multiple conferences. She gave me so much at Grambling where she became my dance mother. I am proud to say that I am one of the male Grambling State University Orchesis whereas for most HBCUs in the SWAC (Southwestern Athletic Conference) there aren't any males in their collegiate dance organizations. It is rare for men to be able to say that they have trained and danced with the women who perform alongside the band and have also put in the hard work and time to be called "Orchesis". Mrs. Grigsby has bestowed upon me so much that there aren't enough words to explain how much she means to me.

My HBCU experience at Grambling State University was one I will never forget. Upon graduating, I was awarded my degree in "Visual and Performing Art" with a Minor in Dance. Then I went on to continue my growth as an artist and persuing my career in Acting and Dance. I've had the opportunity to dance Overseas in Guam in the Zubrick's show where I was a Show Boy. Also, I performed the musical "Aint Misbehavin" in Paris, France, for the France Ambassador. I've been featured on the Lifetime TV show "Bring It" where myself was a guest dance judge alongside renowned choreographer Tanisha Scott and Entertainer Mila Jam. Being able to work with different artists such as Beyoncé, Doug E. Fresh, and Trina to name a few, has been a dream come true. I've taught and worked alongside NBA and NFL dancers such as Miami Dolphins, Atlanta Hawks, and New Orleans Pelicans. I've had the opportunity to dance with Beyoncé at the 2013 Super Bowl. I was in the Production 'YoSef' where I performed in New York. I recently danced on stage in May 2022 with artist Mia X who was a part of the "No Limit Reunion Tour" with artist Master P. I have upcoming 2023 dance Camps with Varsity, which is one of the top dance brands in the world. In the fall of 2023. Also, during the year of 2023 I will be featured in the fourth season of "Why Not Us" on ESPN + directed by Sia Stewart. This is what I have accomplished thus far in my career and I will continue my career in acting and dancing.

I want to thank God above, my family, my mom Tammy Miller, my sisters Kaylan Miller and Kamren Clark, my uncle Darren Miller, my cousin Justin Miller, my aunts Margo Miller and Karen Miller, and my nanny Lynette Greene. I also want to thank the angels that watch over me, my cousin Jude Landry, my Grandmother Toni Miller/Dering, my great-grandmother Joyce Miller. I thank my best friend J'aime Griffith who has always kept me level-headed and grounded. I thank Justin Roberson and my Orchesis big sister Ebony Parson for keeping me motivated and focused on my dreams and goals. Mrs. Grigsby, Teshia Lincoln, Larrlenski Jackson, Tche-Lin Johnson, Jason Roberson, Anthony Cheathem, Leonard Nicholson, Thomika Andrews, Sean Turner, Dawn Clements, Dr. Godwin, and many more who have believed in me on this journey to becoming the artist and person I am today. Being surrounded by many great and supportive people has made my Grambling State University experience one of the best experiences I will forever appreciate.

About Willie Miller

Willie Miller is a graduate visual and performing arts major with a concentration in theatre and a minor in Dance from Grambling state University. He is a Native of New Orleans, LA. He has danced with Grambling State Orchesis Dance Company where he trained in different styles of dance under a former Alvin Alley Dance Company member Mrs. Diane Maroney Grigsby. He has performed with Beyoncé, Doug E. Fresh, Deborah Wilson, and Trina etc, Mr. Miller has performed in Guam and Paris, France. Willie also teaches dance and acting through out numerous states and has choreographed for a competitor of DD4L and also judged for a reality tv series which premiered on *Lifetime. He's worked with numerous of NBA dancer and not to mention that his* choreography is Nationally Ranked by The Dallas Cowboys Cheerleaders National Championship. Willie Miller has judged at different competitions in Arkansas, Louisiana, and New York. I've also judged for upcoming field shows for The Grambling State Orchesis Dance Company. Willie Miller has also travel and worked teaching dance camps for Varsity dance and cheer. He has also performed in many productions such as The Wiz, Aintmisbehavin (where he performed in Paris France), Fences, Miss Evers' Boys, and more. Willie Miller has performed on with artist Mia X in the "No Limit Tour Reunion" with artist Master P. In the fall of 2023 Willie will be featured in the fourth season of "Why Not Us" Directed Sia Stewart. Willie Miller continues to peruse his career in acting and dancing and also travel to teach and choreograph.

BAYONNE R. GRESHAM

A Fair Exchange
Bayonne R. Gresham

My journey to Louisiana is not like most. I was already a sophomore at California State University Northridge; it was a place with which I was familiar, and I was close to family, friends, and everything I knew to be home. Despite my comfort, I decided to make one of the best decisions of my life by transferring to Grambling State University. This decision warrants a bit of a back story; see, the reason my transfer wasn't like most was because I actually began as an exchange student.

When starting college after high school, I learned about the National Student Exchange Program. This granted me the opportunity to attend a university within the United States that also participated in the program. One of those schools just so happened to be Grambling State University. With the help of my friend, I was able to put together an application, and I submitted my schools of choice. Grambling was on that list, and the rest is history.

When telling this story, I am often met with several of the same questions: "Did you know anyone? Did a family member attend Grambling before you did? How did you hear about Grambling? Why did you choose a campus where you knew absolutely no one?"

The answer was simple, I always wanted to experience an HBCU, and, being in California, there wasn't much exposure to them besides what we saw on TV and in movies. Prior to attending, my knowledge of black colleges stemmed from the on-screen portrayals in entertainment: *A Different World, School Daze,* and *Drumline.* Hearing stories of unforgettable weekends at Howard's homecoming and occasionally seeing the Bayou Classic made me realize that it was a world I needed to experience for myself. Therefore, I said my goodbyes and packed my bags for Grambling State University.

I arrived on campus, or I should say across the street from it, full of optimism and ready to see what the black college experience was all about. However, when stepping off the greyhound, I had my luggage and not a single clue of where to go. I could see the GSU sign across the street, but I had no idea how to get to my dorm or what administrative authority I should ask for assistance. Because I was in the South, I was greeted by an elderly gentleman, in a pickup truck, who offered to assist me. Legit nerves and fear set in; I heard a lot of crazy things about the South, and I wasn't sure if this was one of those moments where I was going to be kidnapped and never seen or heard from again. However, with his Southern charm, he assured me I'd be okay, and he would take me to my dorms. He asked me in which dorm I would be residing, and I simply replied "Hunter." He placed my bags in the back of the truck and said, "Oh you're one of those smart kids...". At that moment I had no idea what he meant, but I was willing to accept the help.

As the man drove across campus, I was transported into those iconic scenes I watched as a child. All the while, I was experiencing literal culture shock. I had never seen so many black people on a university campus. I was dropped off at my dorm, a place that I would now call home, and it was surreal. There was a lot to unpack physically, mentally, and emotionally. I did it. I left home, and I started my new collegiate adventure at a black institution. I was left wondering what I would do now.

Everything was so new to me, from the different financial aid process to something called a "fee sheet," and even the cafeteria seemed completely new. I was lucky enough to have a dorm that sat right on the yard. I didn't understand the prime real estate it was at the time, but, let's just say, a time was had in that dorm. Thank goodness I didn't have to go through all of this newness alone, another exchange student was there as well. Tiffany and I were as thick as thieves, and we both knew what it was like to come from PWI's; therefore, we were able to share this experience together. However, Tiffany wasn't the only friend I quickly made at GSU. While standing in line for financial aid, I overheard a conversation that would change my entire college experience.

Many people know that I was a part of the Orchesis Dance Company, and that, alone, could fill its own book with all of the stories from that time of my life. I knew I wanted to be "one of the girls I saw in drumline," but, again, I didn't know how, and I didn't know anyone that could help make this happen. While in line for financial aid, I overheard a conversation, "... all you need are ballet tights, shoes and to be at the women's gym at 4:00 PM..." I was oblivious to what that truly meant, and I was curious. I knew that I never left home without my dance gear, so, that day at 4:00 o'clock, I found my way to the women's gym, and I was greeted by a group of women that I now call my dance sisters.

I knew, when I left California, I wasn't coming back, and my first year on campus solidified my decision. Therefore, after studying French for three years on the collegiate level, I decided to switch majors, and I officially joined the Mass Communications department to study Public Relations and quickly began the transfer process. Grambling would officially become my home away from home.

When I look back at the many stories and experiences that I can tell about my time at Grambling, it always starts with me being an exchange student. The rest is filled with memories I made while on campus that will never be forgotten. We shared laughs, shared tears, had no water, had tiger bucks, experienced break ups, experienced love stories, got straight A's, got barely passing grades, and managed a SWAC Championship or two. Grambling helped shape me into a young, black woman coming into her own. I found the voice that I never thought I would discover. It gave me a sense of pride that I never thought I would experience from my previous college.

Grambling accepted me, I accepted it, and I will always cherish that it is truly a place "Where Everybody is Somebody."

About Bayonne R. Gresham

Bayonne R. Gresham graduated from Grambling State University in the spring of 2009, where she earned her degree in mass communications with a double concentration in public relations and journalism. After leaving Northern Louisiana, Bayonne headed home to So. California to continue what would be a 22 year and counting career in retail. Here, she combines a passion for style with the ability to coach others in an environment that promotes development and professional growth. Currently, Bayonne lives in the suburbs of the Chicagoland Area where she's focused on wellness and living life to the fullest.

GLYNN E. PRICE JR.

Faith To Change
Glynn E. Price Jr.

Senior year 2012 was different. I knew that college was coming to an end, I didn't know what was next. I knew I wanted more out of life but didn't really know what that more was. 2012 one of the biggest movements in the country started and I knew I wanted to help change the narrative of young black men in our country. This movement shined a light on things that our country has needed for years. Although a lot of people would disagree with this movement deep inside, we all knew that it was much needed. This movement would spark protests across the county shedding light on exactly how unjust our justice system is to young black men. This movement would come to be known as the Black Lives Matter movement and because of Grambling State University I was inspired to create something that will help change the narrative and help young black men in our country.

February 26, 2012 was a day that I would never forget and it was a day that changed my life forever. On that day a young man by the name of Trayvon Martin was killed. Shortly after this news the BLM movement was created.

The day after I was sitting in my apartment and I felt the spirit come over me and that's the day I knew that it was time to START my life's mission. That Monday I visited Dr. Fred, one of my college professors who I had a great relationship with. We talked for hours in his office about what I felt in my apartment and my mission to help inspire, mentor and give back to the community. After talking with him he inspired me to not be scared to give my testimony, to not talk about change but be the change. That has stuck with me my entire life even to this day.

Shortly after that conversation with Dr. Fred, I started volunteering/mentoring at the local YMCA. I took this opportunity because I knew that the only reason, I was successful was because of a scholarship I received when graduating from high school. At the scholarship awards banquet I announced that I was going to Grambling. A Board member by the name of David Aubrey pulled me to the side afterwards and said "You know I'm a Gramblinite and I'm going to be checking on you." From that day to now he has been a mentor and father figure to me. So I wanted to pay it forward and not only talk about change but help be the change.

The next week Dr. Fred asked the class to create something that will last for years and that would help create a positive change in our communities. I was sitting in my apartment thinking about this project and I said to myself that one thing I want to do is to be able to create something that will touch/mentor the souls of young black men and teach them to be free and not chained to the stereotype's life puts on us as black men. That was the day I created the "Unchained Life Scholarship".

Once I finalized all the details of the mentorship/scholarship, I created a presentation and, on my day to present I was extra eager to share with the class what I had created. I felt like a kid in the candy store because I had put so much time and energy into this project and it really meant a lot to me. I created a PowerPoint logo and even got an EIN for it. After I presented, I ended it with a poem titled "I Am A Black Man, I Am The Original Man". Once I was done the whole class stood up clapping which warmed my soul knowing that they listened and understood my vision for "Unchained Life Scholarship". During class Dr. Fred asked me to stay after and he told me, "Mr. Price, I am very pleased with your work on this project. I am so pleased that I am going to pay to get your Unchained Life Scholarship registered as a 501(c)3 in the state of Louisiana".

Experiences like this at Grambling State University are what helped mold me into the man I am today. I am a man that not only talks about change, but I am the change. I am not only a man that wants more, I make more happen. Going to an HBCU was one of the best decisions that I have ever made and when I talk to young men, I tell them this story to help inspire them and to become the change and not just talk about it.

It is now 2023 and I have been out of college eleven years and to this day I still have my annual Unchained Life Scholarship. This scholarship gifts kids' funds for college and mentors them throughout their college careers. This is one of my life's missions to mentor and support young men that look like me. I want to help them become better, help them understand life and help them through any trials and tribulations that they experience in life. A lot of kids don't have that at home and having a mentor/father figure can make a world of a difference. I know because I am a living testimony.

Last year one of my first recipients called and told me that he was starting a mentorship program for high school freshmen and sophomores to teach them about money management, operating a bank account and what interest rates are. Of everything I have accomplished in life this was one of the proudest moments I have ever experienced. None of this would have happened if it wasn't for an HBCU and in my case Grambling State University. BE THE CHANGE.

"Unchained Life Scholarship" is still a registered 501(c)3. Visit us today: www.unchainedlifescholarship.com.

"I can't show you how to be perfect,
BUT I can show you how to never give up"
-GLYNN PRICE

In Loving Memory of Mary Jackson

About Glynn E. Price Jr.

Glynn grew up in a small village called Shady Grove, Louisiana about 40 minutes from Monroe, Louisiana and 1.5hrs from Shreveport, Louisiana. He attended Saline High School in Saline, LA, he received his Bachelor of Arts in marketing from Grambling State University. He is currently living in Dallas, TX.

Glynn is not your average millennial. Young yes, average not. He is currently a licensed Realtor in Louisiana & Texas and a real estate investor, former: police officer in Atlanta, GA, project manager for Hertz, account executive for Urban One, INC., disaster relief project manager for Franklin Associate and integrated solution consultant for AT&T. He did all of this by 33 years of age. All of these experiences have one common trait which is interacting with people on a daily. Glynn loves helping people.

At the age 29 his health took a turn for the worst. One day he woke up in the middle of the night gasping for air and was rushed to the hospital. He was diagnosed with congestive heart failure and dilated cardiomyopathy with a heart ejection fraction of 6%. This would change his life entirely. At age 30 he had a defibrillator inserted in the top left of his chest and at 31 he had a respicardia remede device inserted in the top right of his chest. Both devices he will have to live with for the rest of his life.

After enduring some of the most difficult years of his life, Glynn is now healthy and living life on his terms and furthering his mission as devoted philanthropist, and his greatest efforts are dedicated to his non-profit "Unchained Life Scholarship" dedicated to African Americans that are high school juniors & seniors that will be attending an HBCU and his real estate investment company Price Group Global, LLC.

Glynn's personal mission statement:

"I can't show you how to be perfect,
BUT I can show you how to never give up"

-GLYNN PRICE

To contact Glynn about media appearances, speaking at your event, or for questions, email: PriceGroupGlobal@gmail.com.

HEATHER N. SMITH

Raising the Bar
Heather N. Smith

Road trip views filled with road construction and orange dirt only meant one thing in our family: we were heading to Grambling! I remember coming over the hill and seeing the campus from my tiny window. Unbeknownst to me, this place would become my second home sooner than I thought. A fellow Ville Platte native was working on campus and mentioned to my grandmother that she thought I would be a good fit for the High-Ability program. This program hosted students on campus for the summer before their senior year and allowed them to enroll in the summer session. The nerd in me was excited about the opportunity to get a head start. Any uncertainty I had about my collegiate decision melted away as the weeks passed during that summer session. This small-town girl was introduced to a diverse batch of people from across the country that looked just like me. I majored in biology that summer and returned home knowing that would change when I went back. That experience gave me an extreme boost of confidence as I faced my senior year of high school. The confidence boost wasn't in a manner that would be condescending to my peers; it was the security of knowing that I was capable of handling whatever was in front of me. I finished high school as salutatorian of my class, and the only thing on my mind was preparing to head back to my second home, the G.

Unlike other freshmen, my friends and I from the High-Ability Program came in with a familiarity with the campus and hit the ground running. Remember when I said that biology was not for me? Well, I decided to major in computer science. Someone mentioned that computer science is a blend of math and computers, and I have a love for both. Unfortunately, that love would not be enough if I was going to survive my first programming course. The language adjustment with professors took some time, but it was obvious that the days of things coming naturally were over. My previous experience with professors turned out to be a gift and a curse. A blessing because I was not afraid to ask for help, and a curse because, well, you'll have to read on to find out.

I struggled through the first programming course and even thought that I had made a mistake by choosing this major. During one of the many lab sessions, I questioned myself out loud. I heard the voice of a former teacher saying that I was already behind since I didn't start programming in high school. During the early 2000s, our high school never offered anything close to programming and never exposed us to it. During this venting session in the lab, an upperclassman said something so simple and profound: "just because you didn't learn it before doesn't mean you can't learn it now. If you already learned it, you wouldn't need to be here." Once that fact clicked, I welcomed the challenge of this new subject that would become my passion.

As time went on, I would encounter more challenges, and every time, there was someone that looked like me to hold me accountable. Do you remember when I told you that part of having some of my professors during my summer session felt like a curse? Here's why: during one of my English courses, the professor gave me a B because, even though my paper was of A quality, it was below the standard that she saw in me due to my work from the summer session. Another teacher would give me a C on a programming assignment not because it didn't work but because I didn't follow instructions and did more than was asked of me. I vividly remember the anger and frustration I felt when dealing with these professors; however, as I reflect, I recognize the standard that would follow me for years to come.

Another gem I found along my journey at the G was the Baptist Collegiate Ministry that met every Tuesday. This ministry provided a spiritual rejuvenation of my Christian faith as I faced the adventures of being exposed to a vast amount of things while being away from home. Between the great sports seasons and the cold winters, the time I spent on that campus laid the foundation for what was coming down the line, and I had no idea.

I spent every summer during undergrad on campus as part of the Center for Mathematical Achievement in Science and Technology program. Some summers were purely meant to elevate our mathematical and scientific skills, while others were research focused. Anytime I felt unsure about my abilities, the staff, and even my fellow participants, would require me to stretch past any uncertainty, doubts, or fears of the unknown. As the time to graduate got closer, I felt comfortable choosing the safe path for someone in my field. I didn't see the benefit of getting a higher degree in computer science unless you were seeking a doctoral degree and planned to teach or do research. On another day in the lab, another professor asked if I had taken my GRE with a tone that insinuated that not taking it was not an option. This prompted a conversation about the possibilities that it provided, and, before I knew it, I had applied and been accepted to graduate school. Before I could head off to graduate school, there was only one thing left to do: graduate. Graduation wasn't about me; it was more about the joy on my family's faces as they celebrated this achievement. Every emotion and hardship experienced was worth seeing the smile on my grandmother's face (a Southern alumna) as I handed her my summa cum laude stamped degree.

The world was waiting for me to test out the foundation that Grambling State University provided for me. The first benefit was being able to attend graduate school almost for free. At the G, I learned about the lack of minorities in STEM fields and the funding opportunities that were afforded because of this demand. My tenure at GSU was fully covered without the use of loans. The overflow from this funding was used to fund my graduate studies. The reality of this possibility was my speech to anyone that would listen, but the demands of graduate school limited my availability to share at the time.

Graduate school served as a microcosm of the real world for a black female computer scientist. I was the only black female during my matriculation through the program. The first day of orientation felt like that frustrating time in the lab at the G, but I remembered that I belonged and could persevere and come out stronger. The G instilled that toughness in me and, this time around, there were far fewer encouraging, accountable friends; however, I still finished it (early at that). This graduation, like the last, wasn't about me at all; it was evidence for the next person that looks like me that they could do it too.

Remember how I previously said that those professors at Grambling elevated the standard for me? While most people were content with just living and focusing on themselves after graduation, I was not. I couldn't let the knowledge and resources that I had accumulated go to waste. The summer after my master's graduation, I officially launched Grind Time Saturdays (now known as the Grind Time Academy): an educational workshop series aimed to inspire youth to maximize their time, to expose them to diverse possibilities, and to help them prepare for the future. Reaching out to my peers and family, I gathered donations to provide journals and food to engage teenagers in my church and community. The Grind Time Participants are engaged in college visits, museum visits, and lessons about important life topics such as financial literacy, college prep, mental health, art, and more. The light from such a valuable movement drew the attention of the Louisiana governor's office, and we were awarded a grant that provided a three-year partnership to elevate the program to the next level. Fellow HBCU alumni serve as teachers and share their personal experiences with the participants.

My experience at the G stretched me and instilled values that require me to look out for those behind me and encourage those like me to do the same. We owe it to the next generation to raise the bar while providing insight on how to avoid some pitfalls, just as those before did for us. Being HBCU educated isn't just a badge of honor; it's a call to action to make sure that we all grind for greatness. It is an invitation to embrace the distinct purpose that God has placed within each of us. Remember, it's nothing but a "G" thing, baby!

About Heather N. Smith

Born and raised in south Louisiana, Heather N. Smith has a passion for learning that propels her to share her experiences with the next generation. Her love for technology and critical thinking led her to earn both a bachelor's and master's degree in computer science from Grambling State University (Summa Cum Laude) and the University of Louisiana at Lafayette, respectively. Her current position is a lead developer at Cherokee Nation Technologies, where she is responsible for managing multiple web development projects and mentoring junior developers.

Outside of work she wears the hats of motivational speaker, mentor, and educational ambassador, just to name a few. In 2012, Ms. Smith launched Grind Time Saturdays, which is an educational workshop series aimed to inspire youth to maximize their time and prepare for the future. She has a special interest in increasing the minority presence in the S.T.E.M (Science Technology Engineering and Mathematics) fields of study. She continues to give back to her alma mater, Grambling State University, through the GSU STEM Advisory Council Board. The board's mission is to enhance the student experience and assist the university in engaging in various educational funding opportunities and more.

In addition to her career and educational endeavors, she spends time advancing her web development skill set, maintaining a fit lifestyle, and exploring new talents while enjoying life with family and friends.

JOE GILL JR.

Let's Stop Trippin
Joe Gill Jr.

As a proud HBCU graduate, I will always recommend Historically Black Colleges and Universities to anyone who asks. My time at Grambling State University was an integral part of the development of who I am, as a man, today. I will discuss three very important aspects of my time at Grambling, my academics, my athletic career, and my social life.

Coming from a suburb of Dallas in the late nineties and early two thousands, Historically Black Colleges and Universities (HBCUs) were rarely mentioned. College was talked about often, but the schools that were typically mentioned were state schools like the University of Texas or Texas A&M University. The only time that HBCUs were mentioned was when it was time for big football games like the Cotton Bowl and the Bayou Classic, which are both games that feature rival HBCUs.

My first exposure to Grambling State University was when I was offered a Baseball scholarship by the school. At the time, I was unaware that Grambling was a Division I (D1) school. Because it was a D1 school, and pro-recruiters typically looked at Division I schools first, I made the life-changing decision to attend the school once I graduated from high school.

During my freshman year at Grambling, my only focus was becoming the best that I could be in baseball, finishing school in four years, and being drafted to an MLB team. Having fun while doing this was, of course, a must. Outside of professional baseball, I had no plans for my future: no plan for what my degree would be in, no career plan, and definitely no plan B. Then the fall of 2010 happened.

In the fall of 2010, I was set to take an Introduction to Sociology class. All the sections were full except one, Dr. Walter Davis' section. This was the section that NO ONE wanted to be in. He was a Harvard-educated professor that received his Ph.D. in Sociology. Dr. Davis was also known to have the hardest section of Introduction to Sociology, so I was not looking forward to it. On my first day, I was running late, and, of course, the only seat left was at the very front of the class, so that is where I, reluctantly, headed.

When Dr. Davis walked into the classroom, the first thing he wrote on the board was "Let's Stop Trippin." This immediately caught everyone in the room off guard. Dr. Davis' lecture that day was about the alarming graduation rates at HBCUs. Our first homework assignment was to research the graduation rates of ten HBCUs, including Grambling's. What I found out from that assignment was disappointing. Rates were low, but not due to lack of effort or talent. Students just were not finishing school for whatever reason. After discussing the assignment, Dr. Davis challenged us. "Which side will you be on?" Were we just going to come to school, or were we going to graduate? He noticed my enthusiasm, and this began our relationship as mentor/mentee.

I met with Dr. Davis regularly to discuss my legacy. Who was I? What was I going to do with my life? What was I good at? I didn't have any answers to any of his questions, outside of baseball, and this sparked his interest. He began to dig deeper, asking questions about my home life. The way that he genuinely cared about me was surprising. I never expected a professor, someone that had hundreds of students, to care the way that he did. Dr. Davis taught me about intellect and its power. He inspired me to want to be more, more than just a Baseball player. This was the first man that I could remember admiring that didn't wear a sports uniform. He was a Black intellectual, something that, in my experience so far, was few and far between. Ultimately, that led to me desiring to be more. I began to explore law school, business, and education. I eventually decided that I wanted to be in the education field to inspire future generations like Dr. Walter Davis inspired me. This led me to get my master's in education and a master's in clinical mental health. Without my experience meeting Dr. Davis, I'm not sure I would have been able to accomplish some of the goals that I have or change the lives of so many young people who have come after me.

Grambling is a university that has a rich history in athletics. The infamous Eddie Robinson was one of the pioneers of HBCU football being on the map, and, at one point, he was the winningest coach in NCAA history. Most sports fans know who Eddie Robinson was and what he meant to the landscape of college football. Grambling also has legendary baseball coaches R.W.E Jones, Wilbert Ellis, James Cooper, and now Davin Pierre who were foundational for the baseball program's success. When I got on campus, I began to understand the expectation to win SWAC baseball championships and go to the NCAA world series tournament yearly. One of the things I didn't expect was how good the players who were already there would be, and how hard it would be to get on the field. Most of us who make it to college are the best where we come from, so to come to a place where your spot isn't guaranteed is a difficult adjustment.

Throughout my four years of playing, I was able to start a lot of games and play in a lot of games. One of my proudest moments was being a part of the 2010 SWAC Championship team. That team went through so much adversity together. The season before, in 2009, we lost the game before the championship. It was a hard loss because we were so close and knew how hard it was to reach that accomplishment. So, to come back the next year and dominate the SWAC tournament and celebrate our championship with the stands full of Grambling fans was a moment I will never forget. Grambling baseball gave me a "never give up" mentality in all areas of my life. No matter the adversity, if you don't give up, you will be surprised at what you may be able to accomplish.

Socially, Grambling is "where everybody is somebody." This statement is so true if you are willing to explore and meet people. A lot of friendships are created by just immersing yourself in the culture of the school. Joining clubs and student government, going to events, and participating in campus-wide activities are some of the ways to immerse yourself in the culture. The friends I made in Grambling are lifelong friends. We celebrate life together. We do birthdays, weddings, and trips together. To this day, we continue to make memories together.

I was very active, socially, on campus. Being an athlete was like having built-in friends. We spent a lot of time together on and off the field, so, naturally, we became friends. I was active with the organization The United African American Men (UAAM), an organization that promotes brotherhood amongst African American males on campus. I was also active with the Fellowship of Christian Athletes which helps athletes on campus bond over their shared faith. This organization also has a yearly conference that allows college athletes across the state of Louisiana to connect with one another. As a member of the Student Athletic Advisory Committee, I represented the Baseball team and acted as the liaison between the team and the Athletic Director. In addition to that, I was the Male Representative my senior year, which allowed me to represent all male athletes on campus.

One of my proudest accomplishments during my time at Grambling State University was being elected by my peers as Senior Class President for the Student Government Association. Not only did I help make decisions on the University level, but I also had the privilege of being a part of the Royal Court. The Royal Court represents the University at a variety of events. During football games, we sat at the fifty-yard line of the field. We also represented the student body during trips and at university events. One of my favorite events was going to the HBCU Kings and Queens Conference. At this event, Royal Courts from a variety of HBCUs joined together to participate in life enriching activities and seminars. This was an important event because it allowed me to gain knowledge, as well as friends from across the country.

Overall, my Grambling experience was way more than I could have ever imagined. I excelled athletically, academically, and socially. I will continue to promote not only Grambling but all HBCUs. I believe that going to an HBCU allowed me to have a college experience that I would not have gotten at a Predominantly White Institution. I credit my experience at Grambling State University for helping to make me the man that I am today.

About Joe Gill Jr.

Born and raised in DeSoto, Texas, Joseph Gill Jr. is a 2007 graduate of DeSoto High School. Because of his academic and athletic achievements, Gill received a Division I scholarship to play baseball at Grambling State University. As two-year starter and two-year captain at Grambling State, Gill was apart of the Grambling State University team who won the Southwest Athletic Conference Championship in 2010, which provided him the opportunity to play in the College Baseball World Series. Joseph excelled on and off the field. He was the President of the Fellowship of Christian Athletes, Male Representative for the athletic program, and Senior Class President for the Student Government Association while at Grambling State University. In addition to these achievements, Mr. Gill is a member of Alpha Phi Alpha Fraternity, Incorporated.

After graduating from Grambling State University in 2012, Joseph began his career in education. After teaching History and Health for four years, Gill went back to school to complete his master's degree in Educational Leadership. When Gill finished his master's, left education all together to pursue a career in ministry. This career allowed Joseph the chance to nurture passion for inspiring youth.

Gill is a still a member of Concord Church where he is actively involved in the Youth and Young Adult Ministries. He co-leads LIT Bible Study, a bible study for young adults passionate about developing and nurturing their relationship with Jesus Christ.

He currently works for the Office of Student Engagement in the Dallas Independent School District as a coordinator, where he gets to touch the lives of at-risk students, something that he has proven to be passionate about. A hard-working family man, and a devoted father, Joseph currently resides in Dallas, Texas with his wife and one year old daughter.

MR. TYRIE GOODMAN AND
MRS. SAMARA FLOWERS-GOODMAN

A Community of Growth and Good Love
Mr. Tyrie Goodman and Mrs. Samara Flowers-Goodman

All college freshmen's stories start very similarly...

We are traveling from our respective hometowns to congregate in a new foreign place, where we will learn to call home for the next four years of our lives. All of our past traditions, teachings and moral ideologies come together to create this adult that the world, as well as ourselves, have never seen. This is what we call a fresh start. A chance to make our dreams a reality. An opportunity to develop our beliefs, and skills, and create life-long bonds with strangers that have the same starting point as we do, as a new college Freshman.

How do we do this? How do we come to a completely unfamiliar place and start a new life? You do this with your community, your tribe, the people that will hold you accountable when it's uncomfortable. The people that will help you any time of the day and don't keep a record of those times. We managed to form a community, with like-minded young adults who, to this day, are still our closest friends. The importance of community, exclusively at Historically Black Colleges and Universities can't be quantified. It provides a stable and nurturing environment for young students entering adulthood. This community fosters an environment where students can feel free to express themselves without judgment. This is what Grambling did for us, it created an environment conducive to the grace that was bestowed upon us countless times through the years.

Samara and I were fortunate to be able to attend an illustrious institution, THE Grambling State University during these pivotal times in our lives. While at Grambling, we were both very active in various organizations on campus. Samara being the executive assistant to the Student Government Association's (SGA) President and Tyrie being an SGA Senator. We had a few things in common that drew us to each other, which were our passion for the progression of our university and the betterment of all students attending Grambling. During our time at Grambling, we were blessed to experience the full range of being college students. From ensuring our tuition was covered, to finding work-study in a great department or even finding places to eat once the café and express were closed! We were exposed to the election process of running and campaigning for campus positions, leading our respective organizations, and giving back to the students that came after us. In college, there were many late-night study sessions and other social engagements that required our time. All of these experiences helped to shape who we are as adults today. We can't stress enough the sense of community and the importance of creating yours, especially during your college years. We were honored to have been connected with countless professors, SGA and Favrot Student Union Board (FSUB) advisors, counselors, Residential Assistants (RA), classmates, and all the faculty members that watched over us. They cared so much about not only our grades and well-being as students but were also interested in our future post-Grambling. They became an extension of our families. They sewed into our mental and financial health. They saw more than just students, they saw the professionals that we could become. They saw us as Human Resource (HR) managers, lead business analysts, lawyers, pharmacists, and CEOs of businesses. This level of covering and protection is something that can't be bought but only experienced at an HBCU.

As you read, you begin to understand us as fierce Gramblinites that bleed Black and Gold. We are Gramblinites that have taken the unconditional love that our family and friends have shown us and channeled that into the next generation of college students, HBCU alumni, and future Gramblinites alike. We would not be able to call ourselves Alumni without the help of our community sewing into our futures. We believe in giving back, as we are supporters of the Grambling Douglas L Williams Alumni fundraisers in Houston, TX. We have both been recipients of many books and need based scholarships from various organizations. We felt that it was also important to sew into the next group of students. In doing so, we have established a Grambling State University need-based scholarship fund that aids students in both the Business and Mass Communication departments. Like our story, this scholarship will start at Grambling State University, but we look to expand to all HBCUs in the future since we are also graduates of Texas Southern University. For more information regarding our scholarship please visit https://www.goodflowersfoundation.com where our mission is sewing back what was sewn into us!

Along with our scholarship, we both assist our companies with recruiting and development. We understand what it is like to search for careers post-graduation. Oftentimes our scopes can be limited, so we make it our personal mission to help educate and expose students to a plethora of opportunities. We partner with our companies to make sure that we offer a genuine presence, via career fairs, interviews, and classroom info sessions. All of these efforts extend that sense of community.

One thing that we always agree on is the importance of family. We are not who we are without the love, care, and nurturing of our family and friends. We would like to send a special thank you to our parents, siblings, family, friends, and advisors for pouring so much of themselves into us and for helping us to become the people that we are today. We would like to personally thank them for their unwavering support and love! We thank you and we love you dearly! We hope this chapter inspires you to continue to give back and support each other, with #GOODLOVE.

Grambling State University is the place where "Everybody is Somebody". This truly resonates with us because this is the place where we came to be seen, heard, valued, and elevated. It's a place that challenged us both inside the classroom and in everyday life. This is the place where we found our voice and we are continuing to use that voice to elevate the next generation of leaders!

About Mr. Tyrie Goodman and
Mrs. Samara Flowers-Goodman

Tyrie & Samara met in 2012 at Grambling State University, where they were both members of the Student Government Association. Throughout their tenure, at Grambling State, they individually experienced many successes. Tyrie worked for the University yearbook as a student editor, a member of the Gramblinite as a contributing writer and photographer, and served as a class senator for the Student Government Association. Samara was a Campus Queen for Sigma Alpha Pi and Chief of Staff for the Student Government Association in both her Sophomore & Junior years.

While at Grambling the couple's friendship grew over their shared love and passion for the growth of their University and their Hatred for Southern University (ha-ha) while shaping themselves to become the adults they are today. They've experienced many fun times attending classes, late-night study sessions at JTS, parties in the yard, football games, Cash Street, Cain gang, Bayou Classics, Homecomings, and Spring Fest while building the foundation of their relationship through friendship. As time passed, the couple experienced great milestones individually but rooted and supported each other every step of the way!! Graduation from Grambling was inevitable, so once their bachelor's degrees were complete, the couple moved to Houston where they both pursued their master's Degrees at Texas Southern University. Samara, obtained her Master of Business Administration (M.B.A) while Tyrie obtained his master's in Transportation Planning & Management, with a focus on Logistics Management. The couple decided to continue their education journey collectively, and Samara went on to obtain a Master's in Learning Technologies from the University of North Texas. While Tyrie attended Prairie View A&M University where he received his Master of Business Administration (M.B.A)

While living in Houston, TX the couple began to grow into the man and woman they are today. They experienced many financial hardships, life-altering family losses, and traditional growing pains as young adults. Through the trying times, they held strong to God, family, and friends to get them through the difficult days. The couple learned that we go through hardships and trials to build up our characters. To make us stronger and to gain compassion for other people.

In 2018, the couple traveled to Punta Cana on vacation. While on the trip, Tyrie popped the question to Samara at a private beachside dinner. Where she, of course, said yes! Through these individual journeys and joint successes, they were brought together by their love for Grambling, Food (lol), their passion for success, and their love for each other. The couple officially married and celebrated a #GOODLOVE in Houston, TX on October 23, 2021, with all of their family and closest friends.

The couple currently resides in Dallas, Texas, with their dog Cole. Tyrie is an HR Manager of Transportation for BNSF Railway and Samara is a Lead Business Analyst for Caterpillar, Inc. Tyrie & Samara are both ambassadors for not only Grambling State University but all HBCUs!

JARED EVANS, ESQ.

My President is Black
Jared Evans, Esq.

Attending an HBCU in the Fall of 2008 was different. In typical years, the fall semester is consumed with plans for homecoming, Greek life, the band, and if you live in Louisiana, the Bayou Classic. However, from the start of the Fall 2008 semester, there was one topic that permeated throughout every facet of HBCU life: the potential to elect America's First Black President in November. At the very beginning of the semester, then-Senator Barack Obama had been formally nominated by his party as the Democratic nominee for President. The possibility of seeing a family that looked like us inhabit the White House changed everything about that year. At Grambling, all organizations that did community service focused their efforts on voter registration and engagement. All programming centered around the election and how we could get involved. All of the guest speakers at convocation and symposiums were elected and public officials from around the country who focused their remarks on what was at stake in, and the importance of, the upcoming election. On refund day, the mall in Monroe was not only packed with students from all surrounding colleges eager to spend their refunds, it was also full of students with clipboards asking everyone if they were registered to vote.

Homecoming was indeed full of the pageantry and tradition that make it one of the biggest events of the year, but in 2008, the Organizing for Action bus, an arm of the Obama campaign, was a central part of the weekend's festivities. They were in the homecoming parade directly behind the President's float, they held an organizing seminar for interested students and stakeholders on Friday afternoon, and the organizers were a consistent presence throughout the tailgate area.

On the night of the election, we were all assembled in the Black and Gold room, the biggest room and most sought-after room on campus for events. Two big screens were in the front of the room. One of them projected CNN and the other had NBC's coverage. The anticipation for that night had been building for months. SGA had planned that night as one of our marquee events of the year, so we had plenty of pizza, popcorn, and soft drinks. The energy in that room was unlike anything I had experienced in the previous two and a half years at Grambling. Each time a state was called for Senator Obama, the crowd erupted like a Black congregation at a Baptist Summer Revival. People ran around and slapped hands with strangers as if their favorite football team had just made a touchdown. As the night went on, and Senator Obama got closer to the 270 votes needed to win the electoral college, someone started having devotion by singing "Guide me O thou Great Jehovah, Pilgrim through this barren land." One-by-one the crowd around him started joining in. Within a matter of minutes, nearly half of the assembled spectators were having full-blown devotion right there in the middle of the room.

As they were praising and saying "Thank you Lord, please sir have mercy, have mercy father," among others, the polls closed in Ohio and the race was called for President-elect Obama. The crowd immediately went from traditional Baptist to full blown COGIC! People were running, shouting, dancing, cheering, falling out, and crying. It was so loud that I could no longer hear Wolf Blitzer on the TV. We partied, danced and celebrated until security told us it was time to go home around midnight. As we were walking back to our cars and dorm rooms, we started talking about how we had to be there for the inauguration.

Unlike our frenemies from Southern and Jackson, our SGA, which I was a part of, did not plan a trip to the inauguration until after the election, out of fear that being presumptive would somehow jinx the election. The downside was that by the time we started planning our trip after finals and the SWAC Championship (which we won) in

December, all of the reputable touring companies were sold out. Dozens of Black churches, community groups, and civic organizations were also planning to travel for the inauguration and they started making plans in the summer. This left us with very few options for securing buses to take us to the inauguration. We finally found a charter bus company at the bottom of the list and we made plans to sojourn to our nation's capital.

The morning that we boarded the buses in front of the Student Union to the inauguration had a different vibe. Technically, it was no different than how we boarded the buses to away football games, including Bayou Classic, the State Fair Classic, and the SWAC Championships, throughout the semester. However, instead of our usual Grambling paraphernalia, everyone was decked out in their Obama gear. Families who lived nearby came to see us off and take pictures. Parents were filming the entire loading process up to the point when we pulled off. Spirits were high and there was an energetic comradery among everyone.

We hadn't crossed the Louisiana/Mississippi line on Interstate 20 before we exited and pulled into the parking lot of a hotel. The drivers were already switching out. We were confused as to why the drivers would be switching out after barely two hours, it was the first ominous sign that this was not going to be a smooth trip. After we picked up the driver and got back on the road, the ride was smooth, until we got to Alabama. We pulled into the parking lot of a gas station and everyone got out thinking we were taking a bathroom break. What we didn't know at that time was that one of the buses had broken down and we had to wait there until the part that was needed to repair it arrived. We thought it would take an hour, maybe two at the most, but we ended up spending most of the day at the gas station. We passed the time by playing spades, charades, phase 10, and other games. By the time the bus got repaired and we got back on the road, it was dark and we were tired, so most of us slept all the way to northern Virginia.

Since we waited until a couple of weeks after the election to book accommodations for the inauguration, hotel rooms were completely sold out for everything within an hour of Washington, DC. We had to stay deep into the suburbs of northern Virginia. This also meant that we would have to get up extra early to get from our hotel to drive to Washington. By the time we made it to our hotel, it was close to 10pm, and we had to be up, dressed, and downstairs by 4am to get to DC in time. Most of us were so excited that we couldn't even sleep that night. We took over the hotel lobby and common areas with our laughter and conversations. We second-lined, stanky-legged, bunny hopped, and Harlem shuffled for hours. We had photo shoots and group pictures. We fully embraced our excitement and allowed it to consume us. This time together and our pure joy at what was about to happen made up for the frustration from the journey there. I was never more thankful that I chose an HBCU, and that I had chosen Grambling in particular. I was with my family and in a few hours, together, we would watch the first Black President sworn into office.

I've lived in Washington, DC now for eight years and I've experienced all types of cold weather. However, Inauguration Day 2009 was the coldest I have ever been in my life. It was a unique kind of cold. The kind of cold that your body can barely stand. I had on two layers of socks, multiple layers of sweaters, jackets, and scarfs, but I could still feel the wind gusts on my face. The sun was shining but the wind was whipping through the monuments and museums that day. We huddled together as close as we could get near the Washington Monument to watch the Inauguration on the jumbotron. I'd never in my life seen a crowd like the one that was assembled on the National Mall that day. The crowd reflected America. Young and old. Straight and gay. Black and white. Northerners and southerners. Everyone there was assembled to watch history be made. I will never forget seeing senior citizens on their walkers and wheelchairs. I thought about everything that they had seen in their lives and what this moment meant for them, how most of them probably thought this day would never happen in their lifetimes, and how much it meant for them to be there. I reflected on how much it took just for us- able-bodied, healthy, college students- to get there, and how much they- in their advanced age and declining mobility- had to overcome to be there. I was amazed to see them stand in the freezing, bitter cold, to watch Senator Obama put his hand on Abraham Lincoln's bible and take the presidential oath.

For the first time, we truly believed that the impossible was possible- that it was possible for a Black man to be elevated to the highest seat of power in our country. For the first time, a family that looked like us would be residing at the most famous residence in the country. Two Black girls, with skin tones and hair textures that looked like ours, would be the First Children. On the mall that day, with my Grambling family, it was like Black seeing Black for the first time.

About Jared Evans, Esq.

Jared Evans currently serves as a senior policy counsel with the NAACP Legal Defense and Educational Fund, Inc. (LDF), the nation's oldest and foremost civil rights law organization. Jared's practice area at LDF is focused on political participation, with a particular emphasis on voting rights, the census, and redistricting.

During the 2021 redistricting cycle in Louisiana, Jared led the civil rights and racial justice coalition, a group of 16 human and civil rights organizations, in advocating for greater minority representation on all governmental and legislative bodies, including the Louisiana Supreme Court, the Board of Elementary and Secondary Education, and the United States Congress. Jared also led the coalition's efforts in successfully pressuring the Governor to veto the congressional map passed by the legislature that packed Black voters into just one district and lobbying the legislature to sustain the Governor's veto. The coalition's efforts resulted in the construction of a robust and comprehensive record of racial discrimination at every step of the legislative process in preparation for litigation.

Prior to joining LDF, Jared held legislative and policy positions with the Louisiana Department of Wildlife and Fisheries, the Louisiana House of Representatives, and served in the offices of former U.S. Senator Mary Landrieu, former Louisiana State Representative and Senator Rick Gallot, and Washington, DC Mayor Muriel Bowser.

Jared is a magna cum laude graduate of Grambling State University and holds law degrees from Southern University Law Center and the George Washington University School of Law. He is a member of the Washington Bar Association Young Lawyer's Division, Kappa Alpha Psi Fraternity, Inc., and St. Augustine

Catholic Church. He also serves as an Adjunct Professor at Southern University Law Center and is licensed to practice law in all courts in Louisiana and the District of Columbia.

IYESHA S. FRANKLIN M.S., M.Phil.

"My Home Away From Home"
Iyesha S. Franklin M.S., M.Phil.

Packing up: Leaving the Nest

The year was 2008, to be exact. I had just graduated Alexandria Senior High School, and I was ready to embark on the next part of my journey. I learned about the importance of HBCUs at an early age. My mother attended Grambling State University (then known as Grambling College) and graduated in 1974, and my siblings attended Southern University A&M College. Our house was the true definition of "House Divided" for the Bayou Classic (an annual rivalry game between the two schools). I also have a lot of aunts, uncles, and cousins that attended HBCUs. After doing my own research, attending High School Day, and touring the university, I decided that I wanted to attend Grambling State University.

I was so excited and nervous because this would be my first time away from my family and friends. The night before I left, my best friend came over, and we had our farewell sleepover. We cried together and prepared for this next chapter because we were both attending two different colleges. The next morning, my mother, father, and big brother packed my belongings into two vehicles and moved me to Grambling State University. On the ride, my big brother, Christopher, prepared me for college life. There were three things that he told me that stuck with me my entire duration at GSU: #1 Stay on top of your schoolwork and use the resources that will be provided to you; #2 always be aware of your surroundings; #3 you are about to meet people and form friendships that will last forever, embrace it.

Unpacking: The arrival at Exit 81

My first two days at Grambling State University were filled with tears. I just felt homesick and nervous at the thought of navigating this new world on my own. However, on day three, I found the courage to get dressed and step out of my dorm room to explore my new home. I found my way to the "yard" for the very first time that day, and I never felt alone again. I always say that, on those first two nights, I felt like a visitor, but, on day three, Grambling State University became my home. I felt like I was a part of the tribe. I met men and women from all different walks of life. They came from different states and different countries. Everyone was mingling and having a good time. D.J. Chase was on the yard, and it literally felt like a party. Welcome week was amazing, and, when Monday rolled around to start classes, I was ready!

Settling in

The classes were just as fun as the yard at GSU. I remember being so nervous to meet my professors the first day of school, but, to my surprise, they were amazing. They made learning very fun. The professors that I had were very hands-on with my peers and I. They made sure we knew their office hours, and they had an open-door policy. We could literally go to them for academic guidance or even personal issues. They would guide us in the right direction and give us important words of wisdom. The Criminal Justice Department was a family. My professors knew me by name because I would develop a relationship with each one of them. We practically lived in Ms. Conley's office, and she is one of the most amazing professors at Grambling State University. At GSU, the professors are not just your teachers, they are your family as well. I enjoyed learning and being a part of many different academic and social organizations. One of my favorite memories at GSU was the night President Barack Obama won the election. Our campus was so vibrant and full of happiness. Everyone celebrated, and it was a party for sure. Everyone was just so overjoyed, and we were able to express it in the most unapologetically black way and just be ourselves. It gives me chills just talking about it. That was a moment in history, and I was right where I wanted to be: GSU! Overall, campus life was amazing!

I was very active in many clubs and organizations while at Grambling. I joined Black Dynasty Modeling Troupe (a modeling group of GSU students) my freshman year at GSU. I met so many amazing people. I learned just how powerful it is to strut your stuff and be proud of who you are, just the way you are. You are typically taught in today's society that modeling is just for a certain type of woman or man. Well, not at Grambling State University. I remember modeling with all shades and sizes of men and women. Everyone was "owning the runway" and doing it their way. This was beautiful to see and one of my favorite extracurricular activities that I was a part of. I also love to sing, so it's no wonder that I became a part of Entourage Performing Arts Group (A gospel choir at GSU filled with GSU students). I loved praising God with my peers; it was so amazing. I remember we would always kick off homecoming week with the gospel explosion. Just imagine an auditorium filled with young men and women praising God together. It was always so amazing to witness and participate. We traveled to different churches and Universities to spread the gospel through song. I was on the President's list and Dean's list my entire duration at GSU. I was in many different academic clubs. My senior year, I was a GSU Student Ambassador. This was a tremendous honor. I, along with my peers, was able to represent Grambling State University on and off campus. We also spoke to high school students about all that Grambling State University has to offer them.

December 2012, I graduated with my bachelor's degree in Science. I was so excited because not only was I graduating, but I was also accepted into the Criminal Justice Master's program. I felt like a pro by the time graduate school rolled around. I knew everyone, and I was finally moving off campus for the first time. This part of my life came with even more responsibilities. I was working a full time job, I was doing a work-study, and I was a full time student. I was also still active in all of my academic clubs as well as extracurricular activities.

Packing up: the departure from Exit 81

Fast forward to May 8, 2015, I graduated from Grambling State University with my Masters of Science Degree in Criminal Justice. I remember leaving my graduation, getting into my car, and driving to my apartment smiling with tears in my eyes. For the first time, it hit me that I was finally finished with this part of my journey. For the past 8 years, Grambling was my home away from home. I thrived at this amazing academic institution in every way possible. I came to Grambling State University nervous, unsure, and wondering if I would be able to do it. I left Grambling State University as a highly educated black woman with two degrees. I was sure of myself and very confident. I was embracing my natural big hair and my chocolate skin. I am who I am because I attended Grambling. HBCUs are such an important part of our culture. It is so important that we continue to keep the traditions going. My big brother always told me how rich our culture was, but hearing it is nothing like seeing it. Some places just have to be experienced, and Grambling State University is at the top of the list.

My forever home

I am forever grateful for the friendships, opportunities, and experiences at Grambling. There is no place like the "G". The experiences I had while at Grambling State University prepared me for the real world, and I have been thriving ever since. I felt the strong need to continue my education, and I received a Master's degree in Philosophy of Criminal Justice, and I am currently pursuing my PhD in Criminal Justice from Walden University. I believe in the powerful words spoken by Mahatma Gandhi, "We must be the change we want to see in the world." Our Justice System is broken, but it is mendable. Through my studies, I hope to help with recidivism in the prison system. I am so passionate about my field of work because Grambling State University gave me the vision to pursue it. I am a member of Mildred S. Jones Grambling State University Alumni Chapter in Alexandria along with my parents. Once you attend Grambling State University, it forever becomes a part of you. My heart bleeds black and gold. Exit 81 will always be a part of me. Grambling will forever be my home away from home.

About Iyesha S. Franklin M.S., M.Phil.

Iyesha S. Franklin M.S., M.Phil. was born in Alexandria, Louisiana. She is the daughter of Michael and Pamela Franklin. Her early involvement in her church's youth ministry, Upward Bound Program, and numerous social and leadership organizations demonstrated her leadership abilities. Additionally, her creativity flourished as a member of the St. John Baptist Church choir in Lamourie, Louisiana where she ministered to the congregation through songs. Iyesha also sang with United Voices of Alexandria and Ministers of Praise (MOP) under the leadership of Minister Cindy Humphrey. Praising God and learning to put him in everything is how she was raised. Under the leadership of Pamela Franklin, she also is a board member of Jesus is the Reason Ministry by ministering, giving clothes and food to different communities, and serving food at the Salvation Army. In 2008, she graduated from Alexandria Senior High School with her mind set on the HBCU, Grambling State University. Iyesha is a two-time graduate of Grambling State University receiving both her undergraduate and Master of Science degree in Criminal Justice in the Fall of 2012 and Spring of 2015.

Throughout her undergraduate career, Iyesha was active in several different organizations including, Lambda Alpha Epsilon American National Criminal Justice Association (LAE), Sigma Alpha Pi National Honor Society (SAP), Alpha Phi Sigma National Criminal Justice Honor Society, National Association for Blacks in Criminal Justice (NABJA), The Fellowship of Christian Athletes, The GSU Student Government Association (SGA). She also had the honor of being a GSU Student Ambassador. She took her love for the arts to college with her and joined Entourage Performing Arts Group Gospel Choir, and Black Dynasty Modeling Troupe. In addition, Iyesha earned academic awards on the President's and Dean's lists. All of these endeavors sparked the idea of wanting further to develop and enhance her education and be a pillar of positive social change. Upon graduating, she moved to Baton Rouge, Louisiana and went back to school where she obtained her Master of Philosophy degree in Criminal Justice from Walden University in 2022. Currently, Iyesha is pursuing a Doctor of Philosophy in Criminal Justice degree and professionally, is a Senior Legal Specialist for the City of Baton Rouge.

In her free time, Iyesha enjoys reading books, traveling, and volunteering. She is an active member of Alpha Kappa Alpha Sorority Incorporated, Zeta Lambda Omega Chapter of Alexandria, Louisiana. Iyesha hopes to encourage and inspire others around her to put Christ first, always work hard, and believe in oneself. "You can do anything that you put your mind to as long as you give it your best." In all that Iyesha does, she pays tribute to her grandmother, the late Sara Elizabeth Slaughter Cooper and her amazing family. From an ancient African proverb, "It takes a village to raise a child", and her village is big and filled with love and support from every angle. They have all played a major part in shaping her into the woman she is today.

ERIC WHITFORD

HBCUs, the Pride of the Culture
Eric Whitford

When a Historical Black College and University comes to mind, I think about the greatness, the pageantry, and the long strands of traditions that come along with it. Each HBCU around the country has something great to offer in their very own way. Some of those things can be the top-notch academic programs, the geographical location, the exposure of the hardworking Fraternities and Sororities, the athletic programs, and the high stepping marching bands. When I chose to go to Grambling, the marching band program intrigued me to want to know more about the school and what it had to offer.

It is reasons like those that help reel in students from all over the world to get a higher educational experience that an HBCU can provide. Just the vibes of Black Culture on the campus can engulf you with pride when you see fellow students "on the yard" mingling amongst each other or making their way to a sporting event. Even just knowing the history of that campus and embedding yourself in it by becoming an active student on it can be a positive experience as well. Lessons are taught and learned on those historic grounds. Not just textbook lessons, life lessons as well.

When I decided to attend Grambling State University, my expectations were just a bit high. Meaning, coming in as someone who has never visited the campus and only had recruitment pictures to go off on, I thought Grambling was a "busy city", like my hometown of Houston to say the least. Now, I was not a total stranger to Grambling. My mother was a graduate from the 1960's when it was called Grambling College. I remember watching the Bayou Classic every Thanksgiving weekend with her in the dining room asking questions about the school, Eddie Robinson, and of course that World Famed Tiger marching band! Overall, when I first got to the campus, I was a little surprised. With me being a Freshman band member, I was on the campus early for band camp, and there was not a soul on campus walking around. Not even a worker at the time because it was between semesters. But little did I know that a small town with a university that has a big name would give me memories and life skills that I will carry with me for the rest of my days. Being a member of the band and two Fraternities has changed my life to the point that my quietness and reserved demeanor was assessed with becoming a Drum Major for two years and being active in community service and step teams through my fraternal organizations of the Epsilon Rho Chapter of Kappa Kappa Psi and the Xi Chapter of Phi Beta Sigma.

Not only were my social skills put to the test at this HBCU, but my academic skills were challenged as well. The teachers are firm but fair, but that is at any college or institution of higher learning. Educators at an HBCU can not only give you a challenge in the classroom, but they can also give you great rapport to help you succeed in their classroom and others. The old motto of "It takes a village to raise a child" was implemented while I was at Grambling. One of my teachers knew I was in the band and would come and check on me if I had missed class or felt that I was not doing too well with something. Being kind of far away from home can be overwhelming sometimes when you are a Freshman, but when you have people that you've just met look after you as if you are a close family member, it can make your college journey a little bit smoother. Those same teachers helped mold me into what I am today as a successful educator myself. The way they cared for me and treated me is the same way I try to build that positive rapport with my own students for them to be not only successful in my class, but in life. Going to an HBCU to learn how to scaffold with my students as well as with people was something life changing for me. The real world can be a hard place, and me gaining the necessary tools of professionalism, discipline, and dedication from Grambling State

University has helped prepare me for that world, to reap the benefits of being a diligent worker and a persistent person.

Truth is, I would not trade my HBCU experience for anything in the world. I honestly do not know where I would be or what I would be doing if I did not choose to go to Grambling State University or any HBCU to further my education. Remember, all Colleges and Universities are not perfect. So, when choosing your college or University, do not look for "perfection." Look for what fits your academic needs for your future as well as the opportunities you can take advantage of to make yourself a well-rounded individual for when you graduate, and you go into the workforce with your degree. The competition can get steep and deep, but if you are persistent in what you want for yourself and in meeting your goals, you will withstand the adversity of finding careers, meeting new colleagues, and becoming a productive person in this world. Going to an HBCU is something that I will cherish and be proud of forever. Where else can you get the spirit and true comradery of Black Fraternities and Sororities, while attending exciting football games with the bands playing entertaining music and putting on a flashy halftime show, and professors going the extra mile to make sure you succeed in all aspects of your college experience? Go visit or get information from Grambling State University, Howard, Florida A&M, Southern University, Bethune-Cookman College, Jackson State, Texas Southern, Prairie View A&M, North Carolina A&T, Morgan State, and many other HBCUs across the country to find out which one would be a great fit for you to thrive and succeed at. HBCUs are not just for African American people, they are for ALL people.

About Eric Whitford

Eric Whitford was born in Chicago, IL on July 22, 1982 to Paul Whitford and Ruth Ann Johnson. He relocated to Houston, TX in April of 1994 to live with his Aunt Theona Bailey after his Father passed away at age 5, and after the passing his mother at age 11. He is a graduate of Eisenhower High School in the Aldine Independent School District in North Houston, Texas. While attending there, he was a member of the award-winning Eisenhower Mighty Eagle Band. He served as a Saxophone Section leader and the first Black Head Drum Major of their Band Program while graduating in 2000.

After Graduating High School, he took some classes at North Harris Montgomery Community College, and transferred to Grambling State University in August 2001. Being a member of the Grambling State University World Famed Tiger Marching Band had been a dream of his since he was in Middle School. While there, he matriculated in Music Education/Performance. He was a very dedicated member of the Grambling State University Band. He played the Tenor Saxophone, served as a Drill Sergeant, and most notably, he became a Drum Major from 2003-2005.

Being an active Bandsmen was not the only thing he had on his plate. He also became a member of two Fraternities. The Epsilon Rho Chapter of Kappa Kappa Psi National Honorary Band Fraternity accepted him in the Spring Semester of 2002, and the brothers of the Xi Chapter of Phi Beta Sigma Fraternity in the Fall Semester of 2002. He worked hard for both fraternities from serving on the Step Team and doing various community service acts in the Grambling/Ruston area. In the Spring Semester of 2007, he graduated with a Bachelor of Arts Degree in Music Performance.

After he graduated from Grambling State University, he moved back to Houston to receive his Teacher Certification through Region 4 Educational Services to be able to Educate young boys and girls through the universal language of music. He started his Teaching Career in August 2009 for the Houston Independent School District and is currently still working for the District as a Middle School Band Director. He has a total of 14 years of Secondary Education and has various accolades, awards, and recognitions for every Band he has been the leader of.

In his spare time he loves to spend time with his Son Eric Whitford II, his Fiancé Crystal Jackson, and playing Video Games. He also likes to watch Football, Basketball, Baseball, and movies/shows on TV Streaming Services. He is truly a Gramblinite for life and supports his College Alma Mater in any capacity that he can.

KDEJA "KIKI" JOHNSON

Growing Up Grambling
Kdeja "Kiki" Johnson

So many times I get asked "Why Grambling"? Being from the emerald city, people didn't expect me to choose an HBCU. I used to get flustered because no one would ever ask a person who went to Stanford or Yale or UCLA, why they chose that school, at least not in the condescending way we as HBCU graduates have been asked. While some people are genuinely curious as to how a girl from Seattle, Washington found her way to Grambling, Louisiana, more times than not it was asked as if my education from Grambling was less than. I can tell you right now, the lessons inside and outside the classroom are some of the best I've ever had.

I used to use my mom as a scapegoat. She went to Southern University in Baton Rouge and while I didn't completely follow in her footsteps, I still ended up at an HBCU in Louisiana. So early on when I was asked I would answer "oh my mom went to Southern," but that didn't really answer the question. It answered how I knew about Grambling and HBCUs in general but not why I chose to get my education from Grambling.

In order to answer the "why" you have to know who I was. Growing up in the pacific northwest is a different experience than most people have. Washington is very liberal and very open but still very white, for lack of a better term. I can remember one black teacher in my elementary school and I do not remember any black teachers in my middle school or high school. I didn't know at the time how much this would stick with me. But I remember seeing a post online asking about when you had your first black teacher and I had to answer with "college." My schools were predominantly white but there was still a mix of colors and cultures within them but mainly it was European.

There were about 200 black kids at my high school out of 1200 students and maybe 50 of those were in my graduating class. I say that to say, I grew up with mostly white friends but every summer I had the privilege of being around talented Black kids from all around Seattle. For eight years I spent my summers rehearsing for 8-10 weeks to put on a professional musical production. It was during these summers that I felt authentically myself. I was around people who understood the struggles of being a Black person in Washington. Some understood the struggle of being a Black girl in a place where European ideals were still the standard. I was around like-minded kids who looked like me and loved the same things I did. I was constantly chasing that feeling of home and belonging and I just knew an HBCU would mimic those same things. I just needed to find the right one with the right Theatre program.

I arrived at Grambling when I was 21, in August of 2012 after deciding to do my 1st two years after high school at a local college. I hadn't done much in life but work and go to school so this was my first time away from home, the first time I was going to have to grow up and be an adult. Grambling was different from what I was used to. I came across the bridge for the first time and I just saw land as far as the eye can see. Washington is known for the trees and the mountains and greenery and Grambling had none of that. I specifically remember how hot it was when I got there, I'm talking high 90 degrees! I'm not used to that. I'm used to highs of 75-80 max! And the humidity was like nothing I've ever experienced. Not only was the landscape different, but the people were! There were black people EVERYWHERE. I had never seen so many black people in one place before!

When you're around people who look like you, you learn a lot about yourself. Coming into Grambling I was mostly shy and reserved. Although I had years of experience in theatre, having to rely on being myself when I was so heavily influenced by the place I grew up was hard. I had to relearn what it was to be a Black person in America. It sounds crazy but I grew up in a bubble where racism existed, but not like it did in the south. It was a wakeup call moving to Louisiana and getting treated differently in Ruston because of my skin color. I had to learn how to navigate this new life. Luckily when Gram Fam says "Fam" they mean it. I never had to go far to find someone to talk about these tough topics with and everyone helped me. I started to see the differences in the place I grew up vs someone who was born and raised in a southern state. I had the ability to be somewhat "color blind" to race while they were living in a city that still had a segregated high school. I appreciate that they didn't treat me differently because our lives were different growing up. At the end of the day we knew we were all going through the same struggles.

I learned to believe in myself because my friends and the faculty believed in me first. Sometimes I just needed a little push to know that I was enough. Even though Grambling had 5000 students, it felt a lot smaller than that. Everyone knew each other and everyone rooted for each other. Anywhere you turned someone was starting a business or starting a new club on campus. It became a haven of excellence. The arts were appreciated and everywhere you turned you could find something to enjoy. Whether it was a show by the theatre department or an art exhibit or spoken word with Lyrical Quest. We were allowed and encouraged to be young, gifted, and black.

Coming into Grambling's Theatre department I had some talent. I had developed a good base and Grambling was there to hone my skills. Looking back, I will say I was a bit of a diamond in the rough. I wasn't the best but I had such a love for acting that I was willing to put in the work. While auditioning for shows, sometimes I was told no. I'm a competitive person so not getting a role was a tough pill to swallow. I used those rejections to fuel my craft. I had to be better, work harder, believe in myself and what I could do. When I wasn't in a show, I worked backstage to surround myself with individuals who were just as hungry for the knowledge and the skills as I was. I had to become so assured of who I was and what I brought to the table so when I walked into an audition, I knew I was walking out with a role.

All the late nights and early mornings helped me get cast in every show my senior year. By the time Spring 2014 rolled around I knew exactly who I was and no one was going to tell me otherwise. I had become a force to be reckoned with. I knew how to stand my ground, speak up for myself and others, but most importantly, I knew how to live a life I loved. When I speak about where I grew up I always say "I may have been born and raised in Seattle but I grew up in Grambling."

So, ask me before "Why Grambling?" and I'd simply say "My Mom." Ask me now, and I respond with the culture that I walked into on that hot day in August. I tell people Grambling changed my life. To be around beautiful black people who were all working towards the same goal of education and degrees, it really changed my perspective on life. I was also allowed to be fully me. I learned who I was and who I wanted to be while I was there. I moved back to Seattle as an educated, well assured Black woman. I was ready to take on this thing we call life and ready to preach to anyone who will listen to why I chose Grambling State University.

About Kdeja "Kiki" Johnson

Kdeja "Kiki" Johnson is a property management professional with a background in Theatre. Currently, she resides in her hometown just outside of Seattle, Washington. She loves volunteering in the theatre community and will never say no to an opportunity to speak about HBCUs. Kdeja has a Bachelor of Arts degree in Visual and Performing Arts with a concentration in Theatre. She is a proud member is Sigma Alpha Iota International Music Fraternity and Alpha Kappa Alpha Sorority, Incorporated. In her free time, she loves to read, go to concerts, and travel the world.

GREGORY L. JONES, JR.

The Land of Opportunity and Access
Gregory L. Jones, Jr.

Historical milestones, rich traditions, and world-renowned notoriety are just a few common topics that ensue when conversation sparks about Grambling State University: "Where Everybody is Somebody."

My HBCU Experience at Grambling State University began when I was five years old, and I attended my very first college football game. This was not just a typical Saturday game, but a moment that would be celebrated throughout Black History-the 400th career win for legendary coach Eddie G. Robinson. Yes, I was there! As a 5-year-old, I had no idea of the magnitude surrounding this historical moment. All I can remember was trying to sit close enough to the band and see the drumline. The atmosphere of the university, the competitive winning spirit, the roaring crowds, the essence of this community-The Black & Gold! This was Grambling, and I knew then that I belonged here. My parents were encouraging and excited about my decision to attend Grambling. They were both graduates of HBCUs. My mother was a proud Mississippi Valley State University alumna. She was an ROTC cadet, a majorette in the band, and a performer in the woodwind ensemble. My dad was a Grambling alumnus and a percussionist in the band; his primary instrument was the snare drum.

In the fall of 2008, I officially became a Grambling Tiger. On August 1st, I reported to freshman band camp and met dozens of fellow band members who would become lifelong friends. We would spend the next two weeks together learning the fundamentals of the World Famed Tiger Marching Band. Band camp began bright and early at 5:00 AM. After roll call, we stretched, exercised, and practiced marching to condition our bodies for the gruesome, unforgiving Louisiana summer heat. I knew that I had to adjust and learn quickly in order to secure my spot on the field. By the time the upperclassmen band members reported for camp, our freshman class was a fine-tuned unit and making preparations for our first performance.

Band camp ended once classes started for the semester; this meant that I no longer had to wake up at 5:00 AM each day. I was excited because now I could "sleep-in late" and still make it to my 8:00 AM classes on time. I selected Sociology as my major. Some of the best college professors were right here at Grambling! I gained a wealth of knowledge in each course. My academic achievements landed me on both the President's and Dean's List.

The most memorable moment of my first semester at my HBCU was the historic election of President Barack Obama. As soon as the results were announced on election night, the entire campus went into an absolute frenzy! Everyone was celebrating this jubilant occasion. At Grambling, the celebration didn't stop on election night. News quickly spread around campus that the World Famed Tiger Marching Band had received an invitation to the Presidential Inauguration in Washington, D.C. This was a huge honor as we were the only university band to represent the state of Louisiana at the inauguration.

As far as tradition, Homecoming was always a huge event at Grambling. The entire week would be fun-filled with many festivities, alumni events, concerts, and step shows. However, being in the band, our obligation was to make sure we put on a grand performance for halftime. Then there was, of course, the Bayou Classic! This was the biggest HBCU rivalry. Each year, during Thanksgiving weekend, Grambling and Southern would battle it out down in New Orleans. The competition was fierce during the Greek Shows, followed by the Battle of the Bands, and finally the big game in the Superdome.

In the spring of 2009, I was initiated into Kappa Psi National Honorary Band Fraternity, Epsilon Rho chapter. It was a great honor to be recognized as an outstanding college bandsman and awarded the opportunity to serve the World Famed in a larger capacity. As a brother of Kappa Kappa Psi, I joined the band's student leadership program, and, by my sophomore year, I was a drill sergeant, teaching and instructing my fellow band members. During my junior and senior years, I was appointed section leader of the Chocolate Thunder drumline. These were the days!

Another notable performance in which I participated was the 2010 NBA All-Star Game in Dallas, Texas. Only seven band members were hand-selected to perform. Our role was to provide our percussion talents, and the Grambling brand of course, to the halftime performance. This was another once in a lifetime experience for which Grambling had afforded me the opportunity, and I was grateful. At the NBA All-Star game, I had the chance to meet many celebrities and athletes. From performing on stage with Shakira and taking pictures with Usher, to sitting down and casually talking to Swiss Beats while he waited on Alicia Keys to finish rehearsing; I was even courtside standing next to LeBron James, Dwayne Wade, and Carmelo Anthony during their warmups. I could not have dreamed any of this!

One cold December evening after class, I received an invitation to a Founders Day banquet on behalf of the brothers of an esteemed organization on campus. At this banquet, I noticed some familiar faces of other young men like myself, who were excelling and trailblazing, both in and out of the classroom. I knew that I was surrounding myself with a prestigious group of men that focused on Manly Deeds, Scholarship, and Love for All Mankind. After many weeks of studying, and upon successful completion of the membership intake process, I became a member of the Delta Sigma chapter of Alpha Phi Alpha Fraternity, Incorporated. Our chapter was known as The Mighty Lumberyard. Becoming an Alpha meant being a leader and mentor in the community.

My favorite community service event was during my senior year and part of the completion of my Sociology Practicum course. I was granted the opportunity to shadow the heads of various departments within the City of Grambling. For an entire semester, my internship was under the Public Works Department, Fire Department, Water Department, Police Department, and even the Mayor's office. Having this first-hand experience of how local governments coordinate with each other better prepared me for how to handle business and conduct myself professionally.

As a proud graduate of Grambling State University, I can confidently say this institution has shaped me to be the person I am and has blessed me with multiple life changing opportunities. I have met many alumni who are excelling in various industries and have grown my professional network more than I could have imagined. Grambling has paved the way for thousands of young people just like me. I know that I stand on the shoulders of the giants that came before me, and I will always be grateful for dear ole Grambling!

About Gregory L. Jones, Jr.

Gregory Lester Jones, Jr. was born in the rural northeast town of Lake Providence, Louisiana on October 11, 1989. He is the 3rd of four children to Gregory Sr. and JoAnn Hampton Jones. In May 2008, he received his diploma from Lake Providence Senior High School. A proud 2nd generation Gramblinite, Gregory accepted a scholarship from Grambling State University and enrolled in the fall of 2008. Following his childhood dream, he became a member of the World Famed Tiger Marching Band and was the percussion section leader for two years. He was initiated into the Epsilon Rho chapter of Kappa Kappa Psi, National Honorary Band Fraternity in the spring of 2009. To no surprise, Greg was a President's and Dean's list scholar. Through his hard work and academic achievements, he pledged and was initiated into the Delta Sigma chapter of Alpha Phi Alpha Fraternity, Incorporated in of spring 2011. Gregory graduated from Grambling in December 2012 with a Bachelor of Art in Sociology.

Upon his college graduation, he followed the footsteps of many family members and served in the military. He would go on to enjoy a magnificent, life changing experience in the United States Air Force where he served in the Cyber Operations and Intelligence Community. During his military service, he was awarded the National Defense Service Medal and Global War on Terrorism Service Medal.

Greg has made a career in the Cybersecurity profession, serving in senior-level roles in a multitude of industries such as public and private consulting, oil and gas, military contracting and higher education.

Gregory is married to Brianna Andrews-Jones, a corporate healthcare professional and graduate of Southern University and A&M College. They have two sons, Gregory III and Cameron. The Jones Family resides in New Orleans.

DOMINIQUE BROWN

Ole Grambling, Dear Grambling
Dominique Brown

Ole Grambling, Dear Grambling, we love thee dear, ole Grambling…you changed my life.

My first introduction to HBCUs was at a fairly young age through my grandfather, a graduate from Prairie View A&M. I remember being fascinated with the idea of what HBCUs are from the history, to the culture and all that they represent. In 7th grade I made a list of colleges that I wanted to apply to when the time came, that list consisted of all HBCUs. I got my first taste of seeing an HBCU band when I attended the Angel City Classic at the Los Angeles Memorial Coliseum, from that day on I knew that I would attend an HBCU. Growing up, my experiences at school have always been pretty diverse until I hit junior college. I attended a school in Orange County which was predominantly white and nine times out of ten the Black people there were the athletes, that's the category I fell in. During my time there, my mind sort of shifted as cheerleading became a top priority for my future college goals.

My list of HBCUs slowly dwindled and more PWIs were being added to that list but that changed sometime in the beginning of 2011. At this time cheerleading was my life and had been for years, so I did more research on which HBCU cheerleading teams were also competitive teams and Prairie View moved up to the top of my list of schools to apply to. In April 2011, I received an acceptance letter to Prairie View A&M. That same month I was in Daytona Beach, Florida for the biggest collegiate cheerleading competition. That is when I first noticed that Grambling State University was also at this competition. I had a chance to meet and talk to some of the cheerleaders from Grambling and ask about their experiences, from that moment my mind was instantly changed. I thought I had missed the window to not only apply to the school but to also try out for this team. I returned back home to California and applied to Grambling that day, not too long after I received an acceptance letter, submitted my cheer tryout video and found out I made the team! 7th grade Dominique's dreams were about to become a reality.

August 2011 my journey at Grambling State University finally began. When I think of Grambling State, I think of the history and how I am now a product of that history. I'm always excited to see the look on a person's face when I say I attended and graduated from Grambling State University, this name has a lot of weight to it and I didn't understand it until I was on the other side.

The first thing that came to my mind when I got to Grambling was: CULTURE SHOCK! Now remember, before attending Grambling I was one of the few Black students in my classes. So to now be the majority I was more in awe than anything. For the first time I felt like I wasn't just at a new school but I was home. I had to arrive on campus about a month or so before classes started due to cheer practices starting up to prepare for the upcoming season. From the beginning the sense of community and family exuded throughout the campus. Being one of the new girls, I never felt out of place or unwelcomed here. Having my teammates was a huge advantage and I'm forever grateful for them and the relationships that came out of being a Grambling State cheerleader. Grambling is where Everybody is Somebody and we meant that. Listen, if you can make it at a HBCU you can really make it anywhere! This was my first time away from home, living on my own and having to fend for myself. I was surrounded by like-minded people, people that would one day become Black lawyers, Black doctors, Black teachers, Black creatives and creators, that feeling is indescribable.

During my tenure at Grambling I stepped out of my comfort zone and participated in the Miss Black and Gold pageant. I was not a pageant girl growing up, I still wonder why I decided to participate and compete but hey, I'm glad I did it, I became Miss Black 2011 – 2012. I turned more dreams into reality, in October 2013. I became a member of the Alpha Theta Chapter of Alpha Kappa Alpha Sorority, Incorporated. This sisterhood taught me a lot about myself, I became a better woman because of my sisters and my Sorority. I learned how to become one with others, how to be a better person and friend, how to better communicate with people that I was forming a forever bond with.

While on the topic of sisterhood and family, I want to talk about my experiences with my professors and relationships that were built with faculty and staff members. Being away from my family was hard. I come from a small family that is very close to each other and I was scared that I wouldn't be able to do this without them. But, the staff at Grambling became family, they were my cousins, aunts and uncles when I needed them. I know at my community college my professors didn't know my name unless looking at the roll sheet, but here at Grambling, professors cared about you, you mattered, your future mattered to them. I like to think that my cheer coach, thee Terry Lilly played a huge part in my life while I was at Grambling. He's the reason why when it comes to hearing "no" professionally, I don't stop at the first "no". There is always another direction or person that can get you to where you need to go.

I was 20 years old when I got to Grambling and was 23 when I graduated with my degree in Criminal Justice. After walking the stage in December of 2013, I moved back to California and began my career with the City of Los Angeles. On top of working full time, I went on to create an online community on Instagram called BlackGirlDisney with another Grambling graduate and friend Mia White. We created Black Girl Dis, LLC because as Disney fans ourselves, there was a lack of online melanin representation in that space. Black Girl Disney focuses and highlights Black Disney fans, influencers and creators, we've built a strong community and lifelong relationships. Grambling has taught me that if you don't see a space for you, create your own space and that is how BlackGirlDisney became.

"Ole Grambling, Dear Grambling, we love thee dear, ole Grambling." I learned a lot about myself during my time at Grambling State University and did a lot of growing up. That place changed the way I viewed the world, Grambling changed my life.

About Dominique Brown

Dominique Brown is a Southern California native who always dreamed of attending a HBCU. In April of 2011 that dream was fulfilled when she received notice that she had not only been accepted but also became a member of the Grambling State University Cheerleading team. Dominique transferred to Grambling State University after attending a community college in Costa Mesa, CA. After walking the stage in December of 2013 Dominique continued her studies online, back in her hometown of Long Beach, CA and graduated in May 2014 with a Bachelor of Science in Criminal Justice.

During her tenure at Grambling State University, she was a cheerleader, participated in the Miss Black and Gold pageant and was Miss Black 2011-2012 and became a member of the Alpha Theta Chapter of Alpha Kappa Alpha Sorority Inc.

After returning home to CA, Dominique continued her studies at California State University, Fullerton where she completed the Crime and Intelligence Analysis certification program. She is currently employed with the City of Los Angeles where she hopes to become a Crime Analyst. In addition to working full time, in her spare time she has also created an online presence where she is the co-creator of Black Girl Dis, LLC and an Instagram page BlackGirlDisney. She focuses on highlighting Black Disney fans and creators in a space where you don't see many faces that look like yours.

One thing that Grambling taught me is when you don't see yourself represented at the table, create your own table!

TAYLOR B. STEWART

Slight Flex, I'm Really Miss Everything
Taylor B. Stewart

How many people can say they *really* go big or go home in a space where everybody is *literally* somebody? As a third generation HBCU graduate, I must say that my four years at Grambling State University were more than I could have ever asked for from a college experience. Before I say anything else, I must give the biggest thank you to my parents and grandparents because, without them, none of this would be possible.

Being from Columbia, Maryland, I never in a million years would have thought that I'd love Grambling State University the way I do! Never could I have imagined that I could have gone to school 1,159 miles from home and loved every minute.

I remember my very first visit to Grambling State University in the spring of 2013. I was sitting in Grambling Hall with my Grandma Lynn and Aunt Nikki as we browsed the Miss Covergirl Calendar and previous year's yearbook. I can still remember being so amazed at all the organizations that Grambling offered and wondering how I could be a part of it. The part that sealed the deal was getting to meet the legendary cheerleading coach, Terry Lilly, where he talked of the amazing cheerleading program and the Covergirl Pageant, which he oversaw. I'll never forget, before he left, my Grandma Lynn said, "Taylor is going to be on the cover of this calendar one day." I can't even lie; that day, sitting at the table, looking at the calendar, I looked right back at her and laughed like *nope, I'd never do a pageant.* What's that old saying? "If you want to make God laugh, tell him your plans." Boy, they were right.

In the fall of 2013, I began my journey through Grambling State University. I came in with a solid mindset that I have four years to make my mark, make the most out of every opportunity. With that, I spent those first two years really focused on things with which I'd already been familiar: cheering, doing well academically, joining SGA (Sophomore Class President), becoming SGA Chief of Staff, and getting to work with the TV Center.

Toward the end of the fall semester of my junior year, I really wanted to do something completely out of my comfort zone. That November, I saw a flier for it announcing the interest meeting. I went to the meeting, got the packet, and rushed to my dorm room to call my mom. I can remember exactly what my mom said, "Now, Taylor, are you sure you want to do this?" I laughed and said, "yes I'm sure, and I think I can win." Both of my parents wanted to ensure I understood that preparing for a pageant wouldn't be easy, and that this was no small feat.

I had a lot to get done; I had to decide on a talent, get sponsors, and so much more. It was almost like an endless list of tasks that needed to be completed. My immediate, and extended, family was super supportive throughout the pageant process by participating as sponsors, helping with my talent, and getting me prepped for my interview. I'm beyond grateful for my village and all they did during that time.

Of course, after I turned in my preliminary paperwork, I had to call my aunt Nikki & Grandma Lynn to share the news! They were both extremely excited and couldn't wait to come cheer me on that March. I spent the next four months working in overdrive from my platform, to prepping for the interview, perfecting my talent, and getting ready for the big stage.

Preparing for the pageant proved to be unchartered waters for me, I was on a journey that I had never imagined myself in. From finding the right type of daywear, swimwear, and evening wear, it was like a huge conundrum that I had to solve. I was thankful that my village was there during that time, from dress fittings to talent practices, it was truly a group effort to get me across the stage. As the pageant date grew closer, it was almost as if I was living in a dream.

The week leading up to the pageant is where it gets gray in my memory. Unfortunately, a few days leading up to the pageant, Grandma Lynn passed away, but her spirit never left.

Looking back on the day of the pageant, it was a literal blur; it was as if it moved both fast and slow at the same time, if that's possible. All I could think about was that I had prayed and worked so hard for this moment, and that it was mine to take. As we went through the pageant, I was staying calm. I thought, no matter what, I did a great job; I did something outside of my comfort zone. Then comes the time for awards. I'm in my head thinking, "no matter what place, keep a smile on your face" repeatedly. The first award is called, "Best Interview, contestant #6 Taylor Stewart." I can see my mom and nana in the aisle screaming and beaming with joy. Other awards were called, but it was time for the big one: Miss Covergirl. By this time my nerves were SHOT, I feel like I've been on stage for HOURS. Then, the emcee pauses before he begins to read the winner's name, to tell a story. The story goes that, at a basketball game earlier that year, a pageant contestant mentioned to him that she would be participating in the Miss Covergirl pageant; before the story could finish, I could hear my mom screaming because the story was about me. To be quite honest, her scream almost kept me from hearing my own name, but the best thing was seeing her at the foot of the stage jumping and cheering with my teammates. Getting crowned that night was probably one of the most memorable and rewarding moments of my time at Grambling.

I've often had people ask me, "what made Grambling so special?" "Why Grambling?" However, the question is really, "Why not Grambling?" The place where everybody is somebody, is the place where students are sent to thrive, to be bigger than the person they came in as, and to truly become the person they are meant to be. Exit 81, Grambling State University, thank you.

About Taylor B. Stewart

Taylor B. Stewart is the Associate Athletics director for External Relations and Chief of Staff for Grambling State University Athletics Department.

Stewart comes to Grambling from Southern University and A&M College where she worked as the Director of Marketing and Development/ Head Cheerleading Coach.

As the Director of Marketing and Development she spearheaded the Stand United Individual Giving Campaign as well as oversaw all development areas including Lacumba Kids Club, S-Club, and Jags Unlimited. She was also charged with creating digital content for the Department's social media platforms. As the cheerleading Coach she led the Southern University Cheerleading program to a 2nd place finish at the 2021 NCA College Nationals in the Small Coed D1 intermediate division.

Stewart is no stranger to Grambling State University as she was a GSU TV sideline reporter for Football, Men's and Women's Basketball as well as the 2016-2017 Miss CoverGirl and Grambling State Cheerleader. While also in college, Stewart became a member of Alpha Kappa Alpha Sorority, Incorporated, Student Ambassadors, The Society of Distinguished Black Women, Incorporated, and the Student Government Association. Prior to graduation Taylor had internships with WDSU, Reach Media, and the Tom Joyner Foundation.

Stewart is a native of Columbia, Maryland and graduated with a Bachelor of Arts degree in Communications in 2017 from Grambling and her Master's of Science in Communication specializing in Public Relations from Syracuse University in 2020.

CHRISTOPHER DUPREE

Beyond What I Knew
Christopher Dupree

Grambling State University, represents something different for everyone who has attended the great university. For me, GSU represents HOME. A place where I feel safe, a place where I feel welcomed, and a place where I feel like somebody, as cliche as it may sound. As a local from nearby Arcadia, GSU has been a part of my life since before birth. In fact, my paternal grandmother, Lorene Mason (Dupree), and her nine siblings all attended Grambling State University back when it was Grambling College. My grandmother and six of her siblings went on to graduate from the college which led to my great grandparents being honored during the commencement one year. My parents also attended and graduated from GSU, as well as two of my sisters and a bunch of my close relatives. At times, being on campus would feel like one big family reunion, from seeing some of my actual family, to seeing family friends, or simply meeting someone who could tell I was a part of the Dupree family. I think it goes without saying Grambling State University has played a huge role in my life and together, these things and others created the perfect environment for me to learn, achieve, and excel during my time there.

Now I will admit, initially I did not want to attend GSU since I thought I knew everything it had to offer. I mean, I did attend the university's nursery school, elementary school, middle school, and even graduated from the high school. I witnessed Coach Rob get his 408th win, I witnessed President Clinton give the commencement speech, I witnessed a World Famed entertainer perform at the Super Bowl, and I witnessed the G-MEN beat up on that team from Baton Rouge plenty of times in the annual Bayou Classic. However, as a small town kid, I just wanted to have a college experience different from what I had already experienced while visiting Grambling State University. As good as that may have sounded, I would later realize no other university could give me what GSU had already given me, which was a foundation. A foundation so deeply rooted, that I'm honestly just realizing how impactful Grambling State University has been on my life. No, it didn't have the same amenities as larger universities around the state or country, but that's what really made it unique. Who knew this Historically Black College located in rural north Louisiana could prepare me for everything life has to offer.

Once I was finally enrolled at Grambling State University, I quickly realized the difference between visiting and attending the great university. And it's safe to say, I had only been visiting for all these years. Although Arcadia was just a short drive west, I still wanted the full college experience, so I opted to stay on campus. My dorm was the newly constructed Drew Hall, one of the university's first apartment style dorms on campus. To my surprise, my first roommates were a football player, a drum major, and a Nupe. So as you can imagine, I got the full college experience right away. Our dorm was a mixture of School Daze and Drumline if you catch my drift. There were times when I would come back from class to a dorm full of people, all wondering who I was, like I didn't live there. But before I knew it, my friends had become their friends, their friends had become my friends, and all our friends were now friends. They quickly went from roommates to family. Things were going so well that by the end of the semester, we were sharing everything from clothes to cars. Eventually they all graduated, and I got new roommates but the one thing they all have in common is, we all became family right at GSU.

Throughout the years, I've made countless relationships at and because of GSU, that it's pretty hard to imagine where I would be had I attended a different university. My best friend and I laugh about this all the time because we met at dear Ol' Grambling. Not on the yard or in class, nothing like that, we met on campus during the late

90's, at a summer program called NYSP. NYSP connected many area kids like he and I during the summers for fitness, fun, and learning, while exposing us to new sports and new people. He and I later met again on GSU's campus, but this time as initiates of the noble Gamma Psi Chapter of Kappa Alpha Psi Fraternity, Incorporated. We soon became line brothers and later the Best Man in each other's weddings. GSU is also where I met my wife, or where my wife met me. She recalls me being pretty handsome, wearing my bowties to class, I recall her being way too pretty for me and my games. But somehow we had chemistry in our physics lab. Lucky, we ran into each other outside of class and were able to get to know each other better. We both went on to graduate with our degrees in Biology and soon moved off to build a life together. But no matter where we go or what we do, if we have any GSU apparel, people stop and ask, "did you go to Grambling?" We just laugh and reply, "GRADUATED."

Over the years, I've begun to realize that Grambling State University is more than just a college or university, it's its own city within the city of Grambling, Louisiana. Coming over the bridge onto campus is literally like entering into the fictional city of Wakanda, only this place is as real as it gets. iT'S full of its own history, its own heroes, and even its own theme music. It has produced everything from entrepreneurs to CEOs, professors to professionals, artists to athletes, with the list growing daily. Needless to say, Grambling State University has continued to thrive while some may have counted it out. It continues to find new ways to excel while shattering old and new expectations. I feel privileged to call GSU my alma mater because not everyone can, but for those who do, know that it's really America's HBCU.

About Christopher Dupree

Christopher Dupree is a 2011 alumnus of Grambling State University. While at GSU, Christopher was a member of the Gamma Psi chapter of Kappa Alpha Psi and the Biology club. Christopher graduated with his Bachelors of Science degree in Biology and later received his Masters of Science degree in Nonprofit Administration from LSUS. Christopher and his family currently live in Shreveport where he works for the local nonprofit, Shreveport Green, managing the organization's two dozen community gardens. Christopher is also the Founder of The Louie Bear Project, a nonprofit organization that promotes environmental stewardship through upcycling fun in schools and communities. Christopher aims to inspire the next generation through his project's green initiatives while making Louie Bear a household name.

Family Reunion
Breana Lathers

I remember visiting Grambling State University my final semester in high school. It was a very last-minute visit; I was leaving a visit from Ole Miss where I had just received my room and board and official acceptance letter. As we were headed back home my Auntie Chiquita Lathers Butler, a fellow Gramblinite, suggested we visit Grambling on our route home. The HBCU gods must've been working hard that day because so many activities were happening on this specific and unplanned visit. The moment I stepped on campus it just felt right, it felt like home. The café had fried fish and it was soooooo good, ha ha! There were so many beautiful black and brown people all there for ultimately the same goal, to get an education. It was amazing to see how my Auntie literally lit up to be back on campus and be overwhelmed with this feeling of nostalgia. For me this was a bit of a shock coming from a PWI high school at the time. The final thing that sold me on choosing Grambling was the dance department. I grew up watching my Auntie Kiki dance for Grambling State University as an Orchesis and I was always mesmerized by that. Seeing her march through the tunnel at the super dome in New Orleans every year for Bayou Classic was priceless!

As we headed out to end my visit I stopped, I looked at my family and I said, "I want to go here." They were all shocked, "like are you sure?" My response was "Yes, I want to go here. I'm sure." With zero doubt I assured them Grambling State University was where I wanted to be. I think that made my auntie's entire day knowing that I would follow in her footsteps. I know it made my mom and Gran happy, considering they were also HBCU graduates as well.

August of 2008 I would start my first semester as a freshman majoring in Biology and experiencing my first official hell week. Hell Week is literally HELL, IF YOU KNOW YOU KNOW. Lol. It's the time where all the school's sports and organizations appear on campus 2 weeks before everyone else to train for the upcoming season. For Grambling these organizations included, the cheerleaders, the football team, the volleyball team, the band and the Orchesis Dance Company. When I say practice from sunup till sundown, that's what I mean!

My first hell week was a doozie for sure, I was extremely sore from rehearsing so much and stressed about making sure I met the field requirements. I believe it was probably my third day of hell week, we were in class with Ms. Maroney in the auditorium sweating like no other. I was standing by this girl named Ariel who would become my roommate and one of my closest friends. Out of nowhere I saw a shadow of dogs run in the auditorium and no one else saw it, but Ariel! I looked at her and she looked at me like; "I know I'm not tripping!"

The dogs ran by again, everybody was still ignoring it! I gave Ariel that "I'm bout to run look", about 10 seconds later the dogs ran on that stage, and we were gone before anybody had even noticed! Even today we both randomly bring up that story of how we became friends!

So, here at the G things are ran a bit different when it comes to dance. Instead of a dance team we are a dance company where we train and excel in several dance styles. Each week you are granted an opportunity to audition for the field show, which is what you see during halftime on the football field. This is where the challenge came in, my first semester I didn't make the field. However! When Sophomore year came, I only needed my one opportunity and that one moment changed the game! In Fall 2009 I danced at my first of many Bayou Classics. I have to say nothing beats that first time experience. It is probably one of my most memorable and cherished experiences during my time at Grambling. Bayou Classic is THEE game everyone absolutely wants to make. For me Bayou Classic was always extra special because it was home. I grew up in Baton Rouge, La and spent a lot of time on Southern University's campus as a kid. Now this caused a great division in our family, because the Southern Nites reign heavy in my family. It's a friendly competition though.Coming home for the biggest rivalry game, dancing and performing in front of my entire family was a thrill I'll never forget. Everyone is here to see ME! I remember checking my phone after we danced for halftime. I had so many phone calls and text messages from friends and family saying "Bre I saw you on tv!"

I was so overwhelmed and excited I forgot I was sick lol. I was so sick my coaches paid for me to go to urgent care to get a shot the day before the game. Orchesis is truly a family, we had struggles, but we always came through for each other. They made sure I got the best care, because THE SHOW MUST GO ON! I had tonsillitis and it was painful, but when those lights came on it was show time!

It's really the best experience ever! Everyone is calling your name from the stands, and everyone wants to take a picture of you and with you because you are the superstar of the show!

My funniest memory is when I packed two left character shoes for homecoming one year and it was too late to go back and grab the right. If you know Ms. Maroney, she loves to prove a point! She did not care AT ALL!

"Bre! I don't want to hear it, double check your bag next time!"

"YOU'RE MARCHING, and that's THAT!"

The woman really made me march in with two left shoes! That march from Dunbar to the Eddie Robinson Stadium is not a short walk honey OK! My feet were hurting so bad, I was so mad at her I wanted to cry. I never forgot to double check my bag ever again! There's a picture of me with my two left shoes and I crack up laughing every time I see it!

Choosing to be a part of the Orchesis Dance Company was one of the best and toughest decisions I've ever made. It taught me discipline, time management, how to persevere and how to never give up on what I want out of life. It kept me out of trouble too, because Ms. Maroney DIDN'T PLAY!

I built lasting relationships and sister bonds with whom I remain close to today. These are the people who I grew into womanhood with. We share a special bond because there is no struggle quite like college struggle, but I wouldn't trade it for anything. Choosing an HBCU just made it ten times sweeter. Every time I go home for homecoming, that massive feeling of nostalgia I spoke about earlier comes over me like a wave. It's one big family reunion where you walk around hugging, laughing, catching up with those you grew up with and reminiscing on the struggle life and living in your glory days.

The stories and memories are endless, but those were the most amazing four years of my life! I'm so glad I chose Grambling State University, "Where Everybody is Somebody!"

About Breana Lathers

Breana Lathers was born and raised in Baton Rouge, La where she attended and graduated from Woodlawn High School. Breana is a graduate of Grambling State University located in Grambling, La. She received a Bachelor of Science in Biology and danced with the Orchesis Dance Company under the direction of Dianne Maroney-Grigsby. Shortly after graduation Breana relocated to Los Angeles, Ca to further her studies and pursue a career in dance. Not long after relocating to Los Angeles Breana was presented with the opportunity of a lifetime to live and dance abroad in Nanning, China. Here is where her career for dance advanced and really took off. Upon Breana's return to the states the dance opportunities began to overflow. In 2016 she was a featured dancer for several companies and music artist as well as produced and choreographed her first Dance Work titled "Flesh: The Sound of Art Breathing". The work was inspired by the Alton Sterling shooting in 2016. In 2017 Breana held the position as Dance Director at McKinley Middle Magnet School of Visual and Performing Arts. Breana also became a company member in 2017 of professional modern dance company 'Of Moving Colors' located in Baton Rouge, La, under the direction of Garland Wilson. While pursuing dance Breana was enrolled in graduate school full time as well. She later received a Master of Public Health from Purdue University with a concentration in Epidemiology and Biostatistics the summer of 2019. She entered the work field of Epidemiology early 2020 as a Junior Epidemiologist for the state of Louisiana. She quickly moved up and advanced in her career in just under a year. She currently resides and works full time in Nashville, TN as an Infectious Disease Epidemiologist and Research Data Scientist. Breana has several certifications, published projects, open research and continues to push the margin in her field of work to date.

In her free time, she enjoys weekly Pilates and salsa class, as well as reading to kindergartners at a local school in Nashville, TN. She also enjoys traveling, concerts, fashion, family & friends, blogging about food and a good cup of coffee!

One of Breana's aspirations in life is to cater to her love for wine and coffee. She plans to own a Jazz Wine Bar and Coffee Shop as a successful entrepreneur. Breana aspires to one day have a family of her own, but for now she continues producing groundbreaking research and becoming one of the most well-known epidemiologists in history.

Breana Lathers is the only child of educator, Angela Lathers. Her mother is one of her biggest inspirations.

BRANDON A. LOGAN

The Power of Thank You
Brandon A. Logan

Before I share with you the profound impact that Grambling State University had on my life, I must inform you of a transformational moment that I experienced a few months prior to my enrollment. A little over two decades ago, I was going through my most challenging hardship as a high school student-athlete. My team had just been eliminated from the state playoffs in football, and our season was over. Not only was our season over, but the hard work I had put in with my teammates over the course of our high school career had abruptly ended.

This loss happened during my senior year. Feeling dejected and disconnected by the recent defeat, I had to dig deeply to pick myself up emotionally in preparation for my school day on that next Monday. My first class was an elective course that took place off-campus at a neighboring elementary school. Prior to the start of my senior year, I had been selected to participate in a program called PAL, which stands for Peer Assistance Leadership. The mission of the PAL program is to tap into the leadership potential of young people like myself to make a difference in the lives of others.

On this particular Monday morning, I was serving as a mentor to my 5th grade student, Jamal. Jamal was, typically, a very reserved individual, like myself. However, for some reason, on this particular day, he was more outgoing than usual. Dominating the conversation, Jamal curiously asked, "How was your weekend?" I began to tell Jamal about the tough loss I had experienced with my teammates, but before I could complete my story Jamal deftly interjected. He told me that although I went through a tough loss over the weekend, he wanted me to know that I had changed his life. I changed his life because I served as the male role model that had been absent in his life since birth, and he simply wanted to tell me "thank you." Sitting in silence for a few seconds, a new emotion began to take over, and it was a feeling I had never experienced before.

Those two words from Jamal transformed my life instantly. The student in whose life I was tasked to go make a difference, profoundly added a new dimension to mine. While I may have lost an important football game, Jamal showed me about winning in life. Within that moment that I shared with Jamal, I was able to discover why I was born – I unlocked my purpose! I came to the realization that when you give, you get – and I had to learn this through experience.

The mindset shift that I experienced in that moment with Jamal redefined who I wanted to become thereafter. My thoughts changed from me to we; consumption to contribution; and selfish to selfless. I was fortunate to have Jamal in my life twenty-one years ago, and, because of what he taught me, I was able to engage in a purposeful journey through life.

One major challenge that I faced during my formative years was identifying with young men who looked like me, had a background like mine, and were simply striving to become more than just an athlete or a rap artist. After connecting to my purpose, my next step was to choose an institution of higher learning that would allow me to develop holistically. For someone who wanted to play major football and study business in a nurturing environment for Black students, Grambling State University became my top choice. Granted, transitioning from a diversified, major city to a small rural community in Grambling, Louisiana was not easy, but it was necessary for my personal growth. Attending Grambling State University allowed me to experience – for the first time in my life – what it was like to be a part of the racial majority in a community and classroom. Now that I was able to witness greatness at every turn on campus, I became very focused on developing into a more well-rounded servant leader.

Drawing inspiration from my upbringing and aspirations on becoming an effective servant leader, I prioritized becoming a major contributor academically, athletically, and in the Grambling community. I faced my share of disappointments and setbacks at Grambling, but there was no challenge greater than my plan, which was backed by persistence, determination, and the right mental attitude. I was fortunate to be recognized on the Dean's and President's list for each academic semester during my tenure at Grambling State University. Furthermore, during my sophomore year, I was inducted into the prestigious Earl Lester Cole Honors College. As a member of the Earl Lester Cole Honors College, I was exposed to service-learning and research opportunities, which truly advanced my educational experiences. Having the ability to take a balanced approach to learning inside and outside of the classroom was always a part of my initial plan. Another value-add during my time at Grambling State University was earning the opportunity to join a professional organization, Omega Psi Phi Fraternity, Inc., which allowed me to associate with men who exemplified similar ideas and like attainments. On the football front, I was a four-year letterman and was a part of the Black College National Championship team in 2005. Grambling football has been synonymous with excellence since its inception, and I felt very fortunate to have this experience as a part of my journey at the institution.

The people of Grambling State University are principally responsible for who I am today. I was able to become who I needed when I was a child, and, more importantly, I left as a leader prepared to contribute to society. While I do subscribe to the principle of being a life-long learner, my formal education felt complete at Grambling State University, because I was now able to use words to move an idea from one point to another. I anticipated achieving this type of significance in my life because I was unwilling to compromise on the type of individual I desired to become. Today and throughout the remainder of my life, with God's help, I am committed to servant leadership, and I am thankful to Grambling

State University for truly living up to its infamous motto: "The Place Where Everybody is Somebody."

About Brandon A. Logan

A millennial and native of San Antonio who found inspiration at the nexus of business, community, and mentorship, Brandon A. Logan has carved a niche for himself as a social entrepreneur, advocate, and speaker on all topics relating to service, business, and diversity. Brandon's accomplishments have been noted on local, national, and international levels. For his contributions, he has also received personal recognition from President Barack H. Obama, USAA, Essence Magazine, United Negro College Fund, Rotary International, and the United States Marine Corps. Brandon has devoted and dedicated his life to service, specifically in the areas of youth, education, and the underserved population. As the Founder & CEO of Urban Capital Partners, Brandon established people- and place-based strategies to uplift the standard of learning and living in inner city communities. The organization's community-based program, Becoming A Better You, has been uniquely designed to deliberately influence a change in thoughts and attitudes by intentionally targeting four cause areas: education, family support, leadership, and health. Moreover, Brandon has spent a considerable amount of time working to positively reconstruct the built environment, through real estate transactions, to better fulfill the basic human needs and desires of the community. In 2020, Brandon became the founding Executive Director of The Doug Williams Center to create a learning commons and advancement space for audiences to examine the history of race, gender, and politics in American sports. Brandon graduated Cum Laude in three years from Grambling State University, where he focused his efforts on academics and athletics. Notably, he was named Grambling Football Scholar Athlete of the Year and was a contributing member to the 2005 national championship team. Since 2005, he has been an active member of Omega Psi Phi Fraternity, Inc., and his accolades from the fraternity range from being awarded the Undergraduate Louisiana Scholar of the Year to receiving the highly coveted International Citizen of the Year. Brandon has also received the Beacon Award from Grambling State University, Distinguished Alumni Award from Grambling University National Alumni Association, and was the recipient of the Bayou Classic Marines' Excellence in Leadership Award. Furthermore, he is a proud graduate of Harvard Business School's Young American Leaders Program, FBI Citizens Academy, and Air War College's National Security Forum. Brandon has a well-established record of giving his time to the long-term betterment of the community. As Chairman of the 2016 San Antonio Martin Luther King, Jr. Commission, Brandon's efforts elevated the standard of participation for the Nation's largest MLK, Jr. March by increasing participation to a record of over 300,000 people and, simultaneously, raising over $400,000 in scholarships. As the 107th President of the Rotary Club of San Antonio, Brandon's strategy was to address the most pressing issues affecting the advancement of humanity, while enhancing the quality of life for residents. Under his leadership, San Antonio's first-ever outdoor ice-skating rink, the Rotary Ice Rink, was delivered to the central business district, all while raising over $300,000 and contributing 8,500 hours of service from Club membership to marginalized communities during the coronavirus pandemic. After being shaken by the tragic death of George Floyd, Brandon co-created and produced a documentary entitled "Living in My Skin" to help facilitate a better understanding to the community of what the American experience is like as a Black man or boy. This impactful film garnered the attention of PBS and, subsequently, the documentary has aired in local and national markets as a feature during Black History Month. As Tri-Chair of the 2022 City of San Antonio Bond Program, appointed by Mayor Ron Nirenberg, Brandon organized and engaged voters across the community to overwhelmingly pass six ballot propositions totaling $1.2 billion – the largest municipal bond program to date – delivering improved public infrastructure in streets, parks, drainage, facilities, and housing. As previously demonstrated, Brandon selflessly gives of his time, talents, and treasures to benefit others. Brandon currently serves on the Board of Directors at The Najim Charitable Foundation, Pre-K 4 San Antonio, Valero Alamo Bowl, San Antonio Parks Foundation, United Way of San Antonio and Bexar County, and Southwest Research Institute. In 2022, Brandon was afforded an opportunity to become an investor in the San Antonio Missions baseball team. Brandon and his wife, Ryanne, have one son, Bryce

SATIN BIBBS

There's ONLY One HBCU for Me!
Satin Bibbs

As a little girl, I was surrounded by professional athletes (NFL & NBA), actors (well-known movies and tv shows), and musicians in the 80s through the 90s. I always knew I wanted to go to Grambling State University. Seeing these people accomplish so many great things and attending a school in such a small town gave me hope. So many of those people I thought I'd only see on TV were right there in my house every year thanks to my parents who always had the BEST and biggest social gatherings in their home. Back then, you couldn't turn on *Martin, In Living Color, Living Single*, or any well-known movie or show without seeing someone with a GSU fit! If you saw Grambling, you knew that had to be the place to be.

As a little girl, I'd attend every Grambling State University college football game just to see the World Famed Band at halftime, the famous backbends, and all the amazing footwork. I also loved to see the Orchesis directed by my favorite dance instructor Mrs. Dianne Maroney. I'd attend every women's basketball game, not just because my mom, Coach Patricia Cage-Bibbs, was the head coach but a darn good one. I would see the tiger mascot and feel the excitement from the huge crowd that turned out for the women's games. The Team was that good! I would see the men's gym packed from wall to wall because all of the seats had been taken from floor to ceiling. I would see the cheerleaders cheer and do flips during halftime. I think it may have made me even more excited to know I could be attending this university someday, if I stayed focused and set my goal out to obtain all the scholarships I'd need to have a stress-free and full-ride education.

Before graduating high school, there was never a thought in my mind of attending a PWI. Why would I? I come from a family where both my parents were the first, in their families, to attend college. My dad, Ezil Bibbs Jr.,was awarded a scholarship to play football at Grambling and passed up on an offer to LSU; he was later drafted into the NFL for the legendary coach, Eddie Robinson. My mom attended Grambling on an academic scholarship; she became an educator and a legendary head coach for an HBCU with over 500 wins in her career. I just knew I'd be attending an HBCU. There were only three schools on my list that I wanted to attend, and that was Grambling, Hampton, and NC A&T. Why these three? Thanks to my mother being the head women's basketball coach for all three schools and me attending their Homecoming's, I figured whichever I decided would be the best fit for me.

During my senior year of high school at Ruston High in Ruston, LA., I met my goal of receiving a TOPS scholarship through the state, an academic scholarship, choir scholarship to Grambling, and a scholarship from my godfather, Doug Williams (the first Black quarterback to win a Superbowl), to attend Grambling State University, so a free ride seemed to be the best choice. Plus GSU is the place, "WHERE EVERYBODY IS SOMEBODY…with a FEE SHEET." Therefore, I was excited to let my childhood friends from Ruston High know we'd all be in attendance together.

During my freshman year, I was able to meet some genuine instructors like Mrs. Anderson, Mr. Taylor, Dr. Greene, and Mr. Burkes who helped shape my mind in a creative way when it comes to the Sciences. I worked in STEM and in First Year Experience (FYE) under Ms. Valencia, or, as I like to call her, Ms. V. She helped me greatly with coming out of my shy bubble and having to mingle and interact with new and incoming freshmen while having to network with faculty and students of all ages on the campus.

During my sophomore and junior year, getting into my core classes helped me maintain and also meet friends that are now lifelong friends to this day. I was able to join the Student Union Board where it allowed me to be involved with plenty of events on campus. From meeting just a small handful of my favorite singers and rappers (Keyshia Cole, Trina, and Lil Wayne) at Spring Fest and Homecoming, hanging out on the yard (everyone's favorite HBCU experience at any college), seeing all the sororities and fraternities prance and stump on the yard, seeing the numerous food places in the Union come and go over time, and experiencing the food and culture from the "Village" in downtown Grambling (especially Tasty's Chicken (if you know you know)).

Oh, and let's not forget the "kickbacks," house parties, fraternity parties, sorority parties, and DJs on the yard (where a lot of PWI student athletes and students had to attend due to not having those things on their campuses). We were also in close proximity to: The Endzone, The Q-Stick, Club Dominoes, etc. Yes, I partied, but I did my work. Being a biological sciences major was NO JOKE! However, I know that Grambling offered so much more than the well-known PWI in the area did: experiences, life-long friendships, and the homecoming's of a lifetime.

My spring semester of my Senior year at Grambling, I attended NC A&T "Aggie Pride." So I do rep for both. However, my diploma is from THE GRAMBLING STATE UNIVERSITY. If I had to do it all over again, I wouldn't change a thing. My experiences, my knowledge, my friendships, and always having a place to call home will never be matched anywhere else.

Thank you Grambling State University for my HBCU experience!

About Satin Bibbs

Satin Patrice Bibbs, also known as Satino, was born on April 25, 1988 in Monroe, Louisiana. Growing up, she was always fascinated by art and had a passion for sketching, particularly in black and white. She also had an interest in the medical field and considered becoming a dentist. Throughout her life, she has lived in various cities in Louisiana, Texas, Florida, and North Carolina, including Hampton, Greensboro, Dallas, Houston, San Antonio, Jacksonville, New Orleans, and Grambling. She identifies as African American and her hobbies include traveling, watching sports, and spending time with family.

Her favorite travel destination is the Virgin Islands. Satin is a mother to a 2-year-old daughter named Xuri and has a Yorkie named Kody. She is a fan of the New Orleans Saints and is passionate about causes such as helping children in need and the homeless. She has previously volunteered in various organizations and is looking forward to doing more in the near future.

Satin's educational background includes a Bachelors of Science in Biological Sciences and a Masters of Science in Sports Administration from Grambling State University, where she attended from 2006-2010 for her BS and 2012-2013 for her MS. During her education, she won several awards including the highest ranking sophomore, academic scholarships, and Earl Lester Cole scholarship. She has also received training in medical billing and coding and has a certification as an Intraoperative Neuromonitoring Technologist.

Currently, Satin works as a Certified Surgical Neurophysiologist in North Louisiana at various surgery centers. She has previously worked in customer service, retail, and administration. Her first job in her current industry was as a Surgical Neurophysiologist Trainee.

She chose to work in her industry because she enjoys meeting new and interesting people and feeling like she has helped them improve or solve an issue that has been bothering them for a long time. Her job is never dull and she always has something new and interesting to learn. She describes her career as challenging, rewarding, and necessary. Some of her accomplishments include the opportunity to work as a Territory Manager for the state of Texas. Though she is not sure yet what professional accomplishment she is most proud of, she is constantly striving to improve and achieve more in her career.

Satin is unique in her field for her ability to connect with patients and understand their needs. She is able to communicate effectively with patients, providing them with the necessary information and ensuring they are comfortable throughout the surgical procedure. Additionally, her ability to multitask and manage multiple tasks at once has allowed her to excel in her role as a Certified Surgical Neurophysiologist.

Overall, Satin Patrice Bibbs is an ambitious and driven individual who is passionate about her work and dedicated to helping others. She is constantly working to improve herself and achieve more in her career, while also making a positive impact on the lives of others. She is a dedicated mother and continues to strive to create a better future for her daughter. She is a valuable asset to her community and industry, and will continue to make a positive impact on the lives of others.

In addition to her professional achievements, Satin is also an active member of her community. She is a member of ASET - The Neurodiagnostic Society and has been involved in several community service projects through the organization. She is also a mentor to young girls in her community, providing guidance and support as they navigate their teenage years and prepare for college and beyond. Satin is also an advocate for diversity and inclusion in the workplace. She believes that a diverse workforce is essential for creating a positive and inclusive work environment, and is committed to promoting diversity and inclusion in her own workplace and in the industry as a whole.

In her free time, Satin enjoys reading and keeping up with current events. She is a fan of self-help and personal development books and is always looking for ways to improve herself and her life. She is also an avid traveler and has been to several countries around the world, including Mexico, Canada, and the Caribbean.

Satin's future goals include continuing to excel in her career and becoming a leader in her field. She also hopes to become more involved in her community, and plans to start a non-profit organization that will help children in need and the homeless. She also wants to continue to be a positive role model for her daughter and other young girls in her community.

Overall, Satin Patrice Bibbs is an accomplished and dedicated individual who is making a positive impact on the lives of others through her work and community involvement. She is an inspiration to many and will continue to be a valuable asset to her community and industry for many years to come.

DR. KIMBERLY F. MONROE

All Roads Lead to Grambling[1]
Dr. Kimberly F. Monroe

Charles P. Adams
Dr. Jimmy Jamerson
Dr. Doris Carter,
and the Ancestors of Grambling State University,
to you we say thank you and Ashe.

To Veda Wilturner, AB Monroe, Ferrie Mae Harmon, Walter Bobby Harmon, and Bobbie Jean Monroe, to you we say Asante Sana, thank you and Ashe.

At the age of eighteen, a curious and witty Black girl from Southwest Louisiana ventured to a nearby university for a two-day freshmen orientation. After days of feeling unwelcomed, unconnected, and homesick she returned home to family feeling very overwhelmed and unsure about what the next four years had in store.

Just days before her first day of college, she walked into the living room where she found her mother folding clothes and her two brothers packing for their second and final years at Grambling. She stood there, scared yet determined. Carefully, without practice, the young Black girl sat next to her mother, and confirmed, boldly, "I want to go to Grambling!" she said.

The entire living room fell silent and still. It felt like the world had completely stopped. Her mother's eyes widened in amazement. "Are you sure?" her mother asked. "YES," she replied. "I didn't feel comfortable at ULM. I made no friends during the two days I spent

---

[1] This is a revised version of a speech given in the Atrium above "the yard" at Grambling State University on November 4, 2022, during a homecoming celebration for Adidas Honoring Black Excellence (HBE) in honor of Dr. Kimberly F. Monroe.

on campus. It just didn't feel right." Without hesitation, her mother rose from the chair and said... "Okay" and proceeded to assist in the life altering change her 18-year-old daughter decided upon just two days before school began.

At eighteen years old, I intuitively knew that I loved Black people and wanted to be around Black people. I chose to, what some would call, "self-segregate" on purpose and for as long as I wanted. I discovered what the Ancestor Toni Cade Bambara would say that "Black people are my business," and I was determined to make Grambling State University my business.

Grambling, as an institution, was built from the ground up through the act of black self-determination and sentiments of freedom. Like many academic institutions Grambling is made up of the Earl Lester Cole Honors College, Dean's List, and Magna Cum Laude. However, our greatest lessons come from the cultural education that very few are fortunate to receive. A Black education excludes nothing, and nothing was withheld from me as a Grambling student...I had everything.

It was here, in these hallowed and sacred halls, that I was exposed to the diversity and richness of Black and African culture, the history, the stories, the music, the rituals, the symbols, the foods, the customs, and the traditions.

It was here that I was continuously made aware that Black genius is approachable and attainable. The education I received at Grambling ignited my Black consciousness and radicalism and exposed me to a world beyond my segregated hometown in South Louisiana. All roads lead to Grambling. It was at Grambling that I met my first mentor, Dr. Roshunda Belton, with whom I traveled abroad for the first time and learned about the global African Diaspora.

My cultural education happened on the very yard just below us. Where I met a smooth and poetic brother from California cloaked in all things African-centered, and I first learned about the freedom fighter Assata Shakur. On whom I would later write my doctoral dissertation at Howard University. All Roads Lead to Grambling.

The role of the university has been, and always will be, the site of struggles, and where we often learn to organize and advocate for our communities. As a result, it was on this yard that we marched in support of the Black men involved in the Jena Six trial; we gathered wearing hoodies in protest of the verdict of Trayvon Martin's murder, and so many of our fallen Black men and women. It was also on this yard that we celebrated blasting "My President is Black" in 2008 when Barack Obama was elected.

And it was on this yard that I sang, danced, strolled, laughed, cried, and made lifelong memories with lifelong friends. All Roads lead to Grambling.

I discovered my strength and my voice at Grambling. Despite the many obstacles with administration, I was encouraged by history and mass communication professors to speak the true truth.

In October, 2013, I organized a rally on campus during the G-Men football team's nationally recognized protest. As editor for The Gramblinite newspaper, I was suspended from the paper for organizing the rally because, ethically, journalists are only supposed to report the news, not create it. I was able to overturn the decision, but it had already gained national attention thanks to social media and news outlets. I was invited to speak in New Orleans for the College Media Association conference and Dr. Judson Jeffries invited me to The Ohio State University African Studies Community Extension Center to speak about my experience. Roland Martin invited me for a radio interview, but I politely declined. I felt that I was moving away from the issue at hand which was, and still is, the material needs of students and the most impacted communities. All Roads Lead to Grambling.

That moment led my fellow comrades and I to create the "Black and Gold Movement," an underground organization dedicated to addressing student issues at a grassroots level. We created demands and met with the current university president (former politician) and administration to consider ways to deal with student needs. We were centered on student power. As a result, we were targeted on campus. I was kicked out of offices, silenced, and even ignored. Professors who were allies would tell me to "be careful." I was told by a staff member that she was told to "watch me." Apparently, we were a threat, which is how I discovered the power college students and youth have across the country. For it was Malcom X who asserted that the youth are the revolutionary vanguard.

We never get anywhere we are without the work and sacrifices of ancestors and elders. I stand on the shoulders, and follow a tradition, of Black organizers, writers, master teachers, and community people who worked hard for moments they may never get to see.

Old folks, like Elijah, aka "Nature Man," taught us that we have a responsibility; we have an obligation to help; we have a duty to build our community; we have a responsibility to give back. When you help somebody, that's how you become big, that's how you become proud, not by getting things, but by helping somebody and leaving the world better than you found it. If you get, give, and if you learn, teach. All Roads Lead to Grambling.

I grew up in a working-class family, watching my father stay up late studying and writing his sermons, and my mother reading novels, which ultimately taught me the importance of discipline, studying, and struggling. You can't have one without the other. These experiences tied me to Black Studies as a way of life as a child. Reading and writing, for me, was about reflecting reality even when there weren't always the words to do so. I find that we are all trying to use words to create a space that creates something, but, if you want to be a writer, you must finish the story.

When I travel throughout the Black world, whether it be Haiti, Cuba, Ghana, or Senegal, I donate copies of Homecoming in

Tigerland to schools, libraries, communities, and bookstores. I share a small piece of the place that gave me all the tools to go forth and be great in hopes that it will inspire others to follow the same path. All roads lead to Grambling.

My advice, to current Grambling students, is to do the work that your soul must have. To take advantage of every opportunity, and to carry on the legacy and Black radical tradition of our Ancestors.

Grambling is a machine, crafted to capture and concentrate the richness of melanin, music, art, fashion, kinship, and community into the students and alumni. We are the Black Diaspora. We are Black Excellence.

I dedicate this award to God, who has blessed me with these gifts and allowed me the ability to spread them throughout the world. I also dedicate this award to my mother Bobbie Jean Monroe, who taught me the true meaning of love and sacrifice. To my family, who have watched me grow and taught me valuable lessons along the way. To my close comrades of Pan African Community Action (PACA) and friends, I appreciate every moment we can build towards Black liberation.

Lastly, I dedicate this to my home, my village, and my tribe: Grambling State University. I thank President Richard Gallot our visionary-leader, faculty, staff for exposing me to my consciousness, sisterhood, and community.

Thank you for invoking the spirit of Sankofa like every homecoming before, the opportunity to return home, return to the source, and return to my radical roots.

I'm grateful that, at the age of eighteen, I not only chose Grambling, but she chose me. She called my name, and my life was forever changed. Grambling State University, I promise to never make you ashamed of me.

Asante sana, thank you all; I am so humbled to be the Adidas Honoring Black Excellence Honoree and Mentor!

About Dr. Kimberly F. Monroe

Dr. Kimberly F. Monroe is a native of Southern Louisiana. She is currently Assistant Professor of African American History and Africana Studies at Trinity Washington University in Washington, DC. She is a first-generation college graduate and earned a Ph.D. in African Diaspora Studies and Women's Studies from Howard University. She graduated with a Bachelor of Arts in African American History with a Minor in Black Studies and two Masters of Arts in Mass Communication and History from Grambling State University (GSU). She's a Lifetime Member of the Grambling Alumni Association (GUNAA) and is the author of Grambling's first and only children's book *Homecoming in Tigerland*, highlighting the rich history and traditions of GSU.

At Grambling she was an active member of various organizations including Sigma Alpha Iota International Music Fraternity, Lyrical Quest, editor of *The Gramblinite* newspaper, and Vice President of the Graduate Student Council. She religiously performed in the talent and starred in the theater production of "Dream Girls." In 2012, she founded Natural Sistahs to provide a space for women to share tips on their natural hair journeys.

Dr. Monroe is the recipient of numerous awards such as: *HBCU Buzz* "Top 30 Under 30" (2017); Grambling University National Alumni Association (GUNAA) "Distinguished Alumni Award Freshman Category (2017); DC Metro HBCU Alumni Alliance "HBCU Young Alumnus of the Year" (2017); and Howard University Graduate School Graduation "Student Marshall" (2019); In 2022, for her work as a community organizer, author and scholar, she was named the Adidas Honoring Black Excellence Initiative (HBE) "Honoree and Mentor". For Grambling's Homecoming, Adidas HBE traveled to Dr. Monroe's alma mater to give her the flowers she deserved. From celebrating the unveiling of her HBE mural to leading this year's Homecoming parade as Grand Marshal, Adidas also gave her community a chance to see Dr. Monroe's Adidas Course entitled "Organizing for Community-Based Power", which can be found at adidas.community.com.

Dr. Monroe has made presentations and conducted research in Haiti, Ghana, Tanzania, Senegal, and most recently Cuba. Her research interests include Africana Women activism, Black Internationalism, Global Black Power, Pan-Africanism, The Black Arts Movement, Hip Hop and Literature. Her hobbies include photography, writing, and traveling to sites throughout the Black world.

JONATHAN WALLACE

A Play for President

Jonathan Wallace

It was on December 17th, 2016, that I lay on the turf in a Grambling football uniform for the final time. The confetti was falling and the scoreboard read "Tigers 10 – Eagles 9". We had just defeated North Carolina Central University to win the Air Force Reserve Celebration Bowl, the de facto HBCU National Championship, and my football playing career had come to an end. It was at this moment that I started to reflect on the many memories I had accumulated at Grambling since my arrival on campus in June of 2013. Going out as a national champion was the best thing I could ask for! The year 2016 was my favorite year in life to date and propelled me into many more successes in my adulthood.

It all started in 2012 while I was attending a football game in The Hole with my dad Herman. Grambling lost this game to Alabama State 18-19, all because the team failed on three occasions to make an extra point. Having always been a solution-based person, it was at this moment that I decided I would play for Grambling, if I were offered a scholarship. Being a black kicker/punter with Division I talent in the sport of football is very rare, but I was fortunate enough to catch the eye of Grambling legend and then Head Coach Doug Williams, since Rayville is only 50 minutes from Grambling's campus. A few weeks later, Coach Williams and a few other coaches came to visit me at school and offered me a scholarship. It did not take much time for me to commit to the G, and the journey to that moment in 2016 had begun.

Freshman year – 2013

What was supposed to be the most fun and exciting experience, freshman year in college, turned out to be the year that I would experience the most adversity to date. The football team was coming off a 1-10 season in 2012, after winning the 2011 SWAC championship. The 2013 team was set out to get back on the winning ways, but two games into the 2013 season, there was a coaching change. This came as a surprise to everyone that followed the program and really shook the culture of the team. The losing continued game after game, and things got even worse within the program.

Everything came to a head when the team made national news for going on a boycott. Only being 18 years old, this was the most confused and embarrassed I had ever been. Not knowing what the future would hold, I relied on my faith in God to help me get through the situation. Only those who were there at the time can really articulate the issues that we wanted to be addressed. Reflecting on this moment years later, I often tell others that this was when I made up my mind that I wanted to work in college athletics administration.

At the end of the season, the team finished with another 1-10 season and a new head coach, Broderick Fobbs, was hired to take over the program. This was not how I envisioned my freshman year going, but little did I know, it was exactly what I needed to learn what true perseverance was and how to fight through tough situations.

Sophomore year – 2014

It was as if 2014 was a complete reset to my college experience because this is when all the real fun began. Spring workouts and classes were tough! The new coaching staff was settling in and really trying to get a feel for what kind of team they would have going into the next season. The workouts and practices were tough, which had guys dropping like flies. By the end of the Spring, many players that started did not make it to the finish line.

The social aspect of college had picked up and I began to have a lot of fun. I got to experience being on a campaign team for Miss Grambling during the spring elections, attend the probates for the Greeks that came out that semester, and even WON a talent show during spring fest week playing the piano. Offseason as a football student-athlete allowed for more time to do things, and I was finally able to really feel what it was like to enjoy college.

Fall of 2014 was when I really started to shape my unique student-athlete experience. Because of the number of course credits I had by this time, I was classified as a Junior in the classroom. Fall elections were getting ready to take place right around the same time football season was beginning. It was one random day in the café that I was approached by the SGA Junior Class President and Vice President about running for class senator. Knowing nothing about SGA or how it would interfere with me being a student-athlete, I developed the courage and received the blessing from my coaches and support system to run for the position.

I ended up winning the election and gaining access to a totally different HBCU student experience. Going from class to practice to SGA meetings was a grind, but I truly enjoyed being busy. It was a huge help that the football team had begun to turn things around after starting the season 0-4. We ended up going on a seven-game win streak that season and coming up just short of earning a spot in the SWAC championship game, finishing with a 7-2 conference record. A complete turnaround from my freshman year, I was enjoying all aspects of my academic, athletic, and social endeavors.

Junior year – 2015

There was a lot of momentum going into the Spring semester in 2015. Jdub, as I'm often referred to, had truly fallen in love with everything associated with being at Grambling. It was early that semester that the thought of running for SGA President began to creep in my thoughts. I soon realized that these weren't just my thoughts. This was the Holy Spirit speaking to me. It got to the point where I just had to share what I was thinking to some of my closest friends. To my surprise, they were responding to me as if I even had a choice not to run for president.

Later in the spring the time had come for campaigning. Here I was, a football player, running for student body president. This was not what I had envisioned a few years ago when Coach Williams offered me a scholarship, but here we were. My teammates, coaches, and friends came out to support me all campaign week. At the end of the week after the votes were read, I had made history by being the first and only student-athlete to be elected as the SGA president, in recent school history.

As if being a student-athlete already wasn't two full-time jobs, leading SGA did not lighten the load. I had to lean on my support system more than I ever had to before. I am very fortunate to say that they were there with me every step of the way and SGA experienced a lot of wins that Fall semester. That football season was even more successful than the previous one had been, with the team going 9-0 in regular season conference play. We took a tough loss in the SWAC championship game to Alcorn, which left a bitter taste in our mouths heading into the offseason.

Senior year – 2016

As the calendar turned to 2016, my focus was on my internship and finishing out my SGA presidency strong. That semester I completed a 16-week, 40 hours per week internship with the Athletics Director at Louisiana Tech to complete my Bachelor's degree in Kinesiology. SGA was in a great place when it came to impacting the student-body and serving the university. You could feel a different air around campus when it came to student leadership. I did not sleep much between April 2015 through May 2016, but it was all worth it!

With me completing undergrad in three years, I had one season of eligibility left in football. Everything the team went through from January during offseason workouts, to that moment in December after winning the Celebration Bowl etched in my memory forever as to why I chose to attend Grambling State University. That season the team went 11-1 overall, won the SWAC championship game, and I was named 2nd Team All-SWAC. I could not script a better end to my football career.

While there is so much more that I hope to share one day, it is my hope that the reader can see how choosing Grambling was the best decision I made. I left the school much more polished and accomplished than I did walking in the door. The lifelong lessons I learned and friendships I made have gotten me to this point in life and I am glad to share just a snippet of my incredible experience!

About Jonathan Wallace

Jonathan Wallace serves as Director of Administration where he manages the day-to-day operations for the athletics administration office and provides oversight and strategy of all administrative operations for the Director of Athletics. Jonathan has been at Texas A&M University since March 2019, where he served as the scholastic supervisor for freshmen football for two and a half years. In this role, he was responsible for providing academic support, guidance and mentorship to student-athletes while working collaboratively with academic professionals to create a highly effective learning environment with a primary focus on student development.

He was then elevated to Assistant Director for Student-Athlete Engagement in August of 2021, where he oversaw career development and employer relations, served as the advisor for B.L.U.E.print (Black Leaders who Undertake Excellence) that was recognized as the Black Student Athlete Summit Organization of the year, and an instructor for First Year Experience. Jonathan arrived at Texas A&M after spending a year working as an academic coordinator and assisting in the office of compliance at Grambling State University.

A native of Rayville, Louisiana, Jonathan earned his B.S. in Kinesiology in 2016 and M.S. in Sports Administration in 2017, both from Grambling State University. As an undergraduate, Wallace served as the Student Government Association President, making him the first ever Grambling State student-athlete to be elected as student body president. He was a four-year letter winner on the G-Men football team, team captain, and 2nd Team All-SWAC placekicker. Wallace also earned his MBA from LSU-Shreveport in 2021.

Jonathan is a member of Kappa Alpha Psi Fraternity, Inc. and loves spending time with friends and family.

JERALYN S. WILLIAMS MPA, CSM

Grambling Chose Me
Jeralyn S. Williams MPA, CSM

Attending Grambling State University was nothing less than a life changing experience for me. Honestly, it was a decision that was made for me long before I was even thought of. Grambling State University is more than a college to me, it is truly my home. My family emphasized the importance of making our mark on this world to leave a legacy. Grambling State University is very much at the center of that legacy. My grandmother was the first person in our family to attend college. A little girl from Mangham, Louisiana, who grew up picking cotton every morning before school established the foundation of obtaining an education in our family. She attended Grambling State University and earned a Bachelor's degree in Elementary Education. An ardent advocate of education, she commuted for years from Ruston to Rayville, where she enjoyed a long and rewarding 27-year career in the Richland Parish School System as a classroom teacher at Eula D. Britton and Rayville Elementary schools. Even after retirement, she continued to significantly and positively impact the lives of countless students as a teacher at Paul E. Slaton Head Start Center and the Lincoln Parish School District. When my uncle, who she affectionately called Coach Lyons, opened Dan-De-Lyons Day Care Center in Ruston, my grandmother became the Director and along with my mother they successfully educated countless students for approximately 30 years. Their students who have become successful in their professional careers, corporate, teachers, professional athletes, including an executive vice president. Because of her deciding to better her life she set the tone for her children, grandchildren, nieces, nephews, cousins, and many others to further their education, many of whom also attended Grambling State University.

Following in my grandmother's footsteps my uncle, Coach Michael Allyn Lyons also attended Grambling State University continuing our family's legacy. In 1979, he was hired as the Girls and Boys Basketball Coach at Grambling Laboratory High School. Along with coaching, my uncle became Assistant Principal in 1996 and Director of Athletics in 2001. His career spanned thirty years, all of which were at Grambling Laboratory High School. During his tenure as a coach, he was able to instill in his players and students a willingness to work hard, to learn and to succeed. His positive attitude and love for the game and kids were evident throughout the school and community. My uncle was honored many times for his accomplishments on and off the court, he was a man of great character. He is one of the most respected men to ever coach in high school interscholastic sports. He is a member of the Grambling State University Gallery of Distinction and the Boys Top 28 Hall of Fame. In 2016, my uncle began working at Union Parish High School by becoming their Assistant Principal, Athletic Director, and Director of Discipline.

My grandmother and my uncle are two of the most influential people in my life. I would not be who I am without their influence and the impact that Grambling State University made on their lives. There is a playful division amongst those of us that attended school at Grambling where we refer to ourselves as "old gram" and "new gram". I honestly cannot characterize myself as neither because I am Grambling. I did not travel to attend school; I am what many alumni would call a "local." It was truly intended to be a negative term but those of us that identified with it welcomed being called a local with pride and honor. I grew up unknowingly surrounded by trailblazers, legends, and historical figures. I say unknowingly because when you grow up around an HBCU campus those individuals are more than their titles and accolades they are family members, friends' parents, or neighbors. You see them at church and when you go shopping at the local grocery stores. I did not grow up longing to see successful people that looked like me because I was literally surrounded by excellence daily. Growing up I did not know how blessed I was. I honestly feel like we took so much for granted unknowingly. We always knew what Juneteenth was, as it was celebrated on the campus and in our community along with many other things about black culture. Seeing black own businesses, black beauty and black expressions were the norm. Black success was not a foreign concept but an expectation.

I can speak for myself and so many other "locals" by saying that we always knew we could be anything we wanted to be and there were no limitations to the greatness we could achieve. That belief in self is a byproduct of Grambling State University. I always jokingly say that I did not choose Grambling, but Grambling chose me, but it's the truth. I did not desire to attend Grambling once I reached my senior year of high school, I desired to go to school out of state. But life has a sense of humor, and my mom basically told me I was staying home. I was so focused on leaving my small community to see the world that I did not realize that by attending Grambling the world would literally be brought to me. I was afforded any and every opportunity I could imagine while attending college at Grambling. If I missed out on something it was simply because I desired to, not because the opportunity was not available. I was involved in numerous clubs and organizations such as SGA, FSUB, Biology Club and Political Science Club just to name a few. Not to mention Greek life, I was so elated when I became a member of Alpha Kappa Alpha. One of my fondest memories was being able to speak with one of my grandmothers' good friends who happened to be one of the charter members of our chapter, Alpha Theta. I was able to let her know I was a member and interview her. She was so sweet and full of so much wisdom. I was also able to meet countless celebrities, athletes, and black leaders while in school, which was pretty much the standard and expected. From travel, conferences, television, movies, internships and so many other opportunities attending Grambling was basically a life hack.

I was also exposed to so many different cultures and outlooks on life due to having professors and cohorts from all over the world. I cannot even begin to recount the lifetime connections and friendships I cultivated while attending Grambling. Professors were more than professors they were and to this day are second parents. They are lifetime connections that I can call on and rely on to this day. These professors are people that will be and have been a shoulder to lean on, individuals that I could not imagine doing life without. One day we were sitting on the yard together laughing, going to homecoming, staying up studying, going to parties and the next thing you know we are professionals, parents, and industry leaders. I may not have chosen Grambling State University initially, but I needed Grambling State University more than I knew. I grew up on that campus as a little girl, walked onto that campus as a naive young lady and walked across that stage as an enlightened young woman ready to take the world by storm. As an adult I advocate for Grambling State University and return as frequently as I can. Grambling has always and will forever be home for me. I graduated from "The Place Where Everybody is Somebody", with a BA in Political Science and a Master's in Public Administration. From the little girl that was once Little Miss GSU to the adult that was transformed and molded by that great institution, I can truly say that I love thee dear old Grambling and I am forever grateful to have been chosen by the G.

About Jeralyn S. Williams MPA, CSM

Jeralyn S. Williams is a native of Ruston, Louisiana and currently resides in Houston, Texas, with her beautiful daughter Jurnee Dior whom she adores. She considers herself to be rather adventurous and enjoys reading, writing, traveling, fashion and spending time with her close friends and family. A graduate of Grambling State University, she is a member of Alpha Kappa Alpha Sorority, Inc. and has a BA in Political Science and a Master's in Public Administration. She currently works in the insurance field and has seven plus years of experience in mental health and management. Jeralyn is the owner of JShondrelle, LLC, an online boutique, where she enjoys self-expression through her love of fashion. As a published author, Jeralyn is truly honored to be part of such an historical anthology celebrating the culture that is Historically Black Colleges and Universities.

ROBERT COLEMAN

The Many Hats of a Grambling Graduate
Robert Coleman

August 1, 2010, might as well be tattooed on my heart because it is a day I will never forget. It was the first day I stepped foot on the campus of Grambling State University, and my life changed for the better. August 1 was also monumental for me because it was the first day of band camp with the World Famed Tiger Marching Band. I received a P1 band scholarship a few months prior during my last semester of high school, and, about a month later, I received a letter saying to report to campus. It's safe to say that the band program was the very reason I enrolled at GSU.

I was nervous, anxious, and excited as I said my goodbyes to my mother, and, almost immediately, it felt like I had become an adult. Band camp started 10 minutes after my mother drove off, and there was no going back now. Before joining Grambling's band, I had eight years of experience in Duncanville ISD band programs. Duncanville's music department was classical, and the marching band was Corp style, so it was a significant adjustment and cultural shock joining Grambling's show-style band. I had to learn how to dance and play my instrument simultaneously, and I didn't have long to learn. I also had to get adjusted to the HBCU band lifestyle. My only prior knowledge about HBCU bands was from the movies I watched growing up. Although those movies did give me a heads up, there was a lot that the film didn't show, and there was a lot that I had to live with every day. Our marching band program is military based and very traditional. I had to learn how not to retaliate when someone is giving you a command in a tone that's not welcoming, and I also had to learn the music at a faster rate than I was used to coming from Duncanville. The fundamentals I learned that semester stuck with me throughout my duration at Grambling and into my daily life as an adult after college.

In my first semester at Grambling, I focused all my time on band and my studies. As a biology major, I knew that I would only graduate on time by staying on top of my schoolwork. The band staff also preached that we came to college for a degree, and everything else, including the band, came second. The band was a close second because this program funded most of my education, and I knew the legacy I had to uphold as a part of it. I still remember how excited I was to perform my first halftime show, my first Cotton Bowl Classic, my first Bayou Classic, and marching in President Barack Obama's 2012 inauguration parade. I was honored and proud to be a part of history marching for President Obama. I will never forget it.

The first semester came to an end, and I knew Grambling had my entire heart, and I wanted to see what else I could be a part of. As I discovered the man I was becoming, I started to get active on campus and, in turn, found out that I was a leader. The fraternities, as well as the other organizations I joined, quickly put me into leadership roles, and, to my surprise, I did well. I joined Kappa Kappa Psi National Honorary Band Fraternity in the spring of 2011. Brand new to the organization, my brothers voted me the chapter's treasurer. The following year and every year until I graduated, I was voted as the chapter's president.

As president, I was also honored to be Dean of Pledges to a new group of boys in the Spring of 2013. As I realized it was more on Grambling's campus than the band and studies, I also joined the Favrot Student Union Board (FSUB) to make more connections around campus and have a voice outside of the band. Joining FSUB was one of the best decisions I made while a student on campus. I learned it is not about what you know but about whom you know while in this organization. I got to work with like-minded student leaders and host events like homecoming, tiger fest, and many more.

The following semester and every semester until I graduated, I was voted Chair of the Lagniappe Committee on FSUB.

As a chair of the FUSB, I was responsible for hosting and being part of all the events on campus. I had the best time while being a member and made some lifelong friends in the process. The leadership role that solidified my abilities and that I'm most proud of was becoming a drum major for the Tiger Marching Band in my senior year, 2013-2014. To this day, I still think "no way" when I reflect on my time as a drum major. I auditioned for a spot for the entire summer of 2013. I was heavier than allowed to be a drum major, so I worked out and got into the best shape of my life before I returned to audition for the directors in person. Seven guys auditioned that year for four spots, and I knew I would do whatever it took to be one of the four. Our first game was the last weekend in August, and I remember my director not telling us which four guys made it until the day of the game. Besides getting the news that I passed all my finals and would be graduating on time, getting the information that I made drum major was incredible and was almost just as exciting. I earned that title and was proud to be one of the few who could say they led the World Famed Tiger Marching Band. To say that I was an ambassador for this illustrious organization and university is something that I will always cherish.

As cliche as it sounds, I am still determining who, or where, I would be today if it were not for Grambling State University. This school has been the foundation of my manhood and my finding myself. I left Grambling knowing I could take on the world; I was a natural leader, and I could do anything I wanted to do if I worked hard enough for it. My education at Grambling has proven that HBCU curriculums are just as effective as any other school and that HBCUs matter. Grambling is my home away from home; every time I return, I am reminded of it. If I had to do it again, I would still choose Grambling State University.

About Robert Coleman

Robert Coleman is from Dallas, Texas. After graduating from Duncanville High School in 2010, he accepted a marching band scholarship to attend Grambling State University (GSU). Robert studied biological science at GSU and tried to be as involved on campus as possible, given his busy schedule. He was a member of the Favrot Student Union Board (FSUB) while attending GSU. He also served as the chair and co-chair of the Lagniappe committee, President of the Kappa Kappa Psi National Honorary Band Fraternity, and Drum Major for the renowned Tiger Marching Band during his senior year.

In the spring of 2014, Robert graduated from GSU with a bachelor's degree, becoming the first member of his family to do so. He joined Alpha Phi Alpha Fraternity Incorporated in the fall of 2014 and enrolled at the University of Louisiana at Monroe (ULM) the following semester to pursue a major in their Medical Laboratory Science program. In the fall of 2017, he graduated from ULM with a bachelor's degree and started working as a medical laboratory scientist.

The results of his labor are paying off as he works at one of America's most renowned medical laboratories. Robert is currently enrolled in a Master of Public Health program to switch to the healthcare industry's public health department or corporate side of a medical laboratory. He will always have a special place in his heart for Grambling State University and the Tiger Marching Band. As cliche as it may sound, Robert does not know where he would be without Grambling State University.

According to RP Podcast
CEO/Founder: Ritha Pierre, Esq.
@accordingtorp
accordingtorp@gmail.com

ACTIVate
CEO/Founder: Yladera Drummond, J.D.
contact@activateleadership.org
info@yladeradrummond.com
www.yladeradrummond.com
www.activateleadership.org

AC Events
The Luxury Planning Experience
CEO/Founder: Amy Agbottah
amy@amycynthiaevents.com

AD Bonner Music

CEO/Founder: Adrain Bonner

817-300-3995

adbonnermusic@gmail.com

Alexander G. Events

CEO/Founder: Nathan Alexander Kemp

Nathan A. Kemp, 336-706-1422

Brooke G. Kemp, 336-944-4768

alexgevents20@gmail.com

Allen Financial Solutions

CEO/Founder: Jay Allen

@jay83allen

@Jay Allen

allen.jonathan83@gmail.com

The Alli Group, LLC
Real Estate Management

Founders: Lawrence & Nickia Alli

@thealligroupllc

nickia.alli@gmail.com

www.thealligroupllc.com

AMMEA

President: Ernest Stackhouse

ej.stackhouse@gmail.com

www.ammea.org

The Ancestor Key

CEO/Founder: Ja'el Gordon

504-356-1466

theancestor@gmail.com

Ashley Little Enterprises, LLC

CEO/Founder: Dr. Ashley Little

@_ashleyalittle

@Ashley Little

aalittle08@gmail.com

www.ashleylittleenterprises.com

The Self-care Doc

CEO/Founder:

Dr. Raushannah Johnson-Verwayne
*Licensed Clinical Psychologist &
Wellness Coach*

@Ask Dr RJ

@Ask Dr RJ

www.AskDrRJ.com

Assurance Tax & Accounting Group, LLC

CEO/Founder:

Kimberlee Collins-Walker

8676 Goodwood Blvd., Ste. 102

Baton Rouge, LA 70876

225-757-7518

kim@assurancetaxbr.com

www.assurancetaxbr.com

Baker & Baker Realty, LLC

CEO/Founder: Christopher Baker

@seedougieblake

@Christopher D. Baker

baker.christopher@gmail.com

Balance Candle Bar

CEO/Founder: Lacey B. Evans

www.shopbalanceco.com

Bald Guys Bake, LLC

CEO/Founder: Torey Searcy

info@baldguysbake.com

www.baldguysbake.com

Beautiful Body & More, LLC

CEO/Founder: Melody Scott

318-716-1507
318-716-1508 fax

@Beautifulbodyandmore

@Beautiful Body & More, LLC

www.beautifulbodyandmore.com

The Black Techies/Podcast

CEO/Founder: Herbert L. Seward, III

Where black culture meets the world of technology.

www.theblacktechies.com

BLKWOMENHUSTLE

CEO/Founder: Lashawn Dreher

@blkwomenhustle

@Blk Women Hustle

info@blkwomenhustle.com

Block Band Music & Publishing, LLC

CEO/Founder: D. Rashad Watters

919-698-2560

blockbandmusic@gmail.com

Boardroom Brand, LLC

CEO/Founder: Samuel Brown, III

@_gxxdy

samuel.brown.three@gmail.com

Booked Cafe Books

CEO/Founder: Kierra Jones

@Booked Cafe Books

@Booked Cafe Books

contact@bookedcafebooks.com

www.bookedcafebooks.com

Bound By Conscious Concepts

CEO/Founder: Kathryn Lomax

@msklovibes223

@Klo-Kathryn Lomax

972-638-9823

klomax@bbconcepts.com

Brooks Art Collective

CEO/Founder: LaToya Brooks

@brooksartcollective

@brooksartcollective

brooksartcollective@gmail.com

BZAR STUDIOZ

CEO/Founder: Steven Baltazar

bzarstudioz@gmail.com

www www.bzarstudioz.com

Caleb T. Dunbar Photography

CEO/Founder: Caleb T. Dunbar

@calebtdunbarphotography

@Caleb T. Dunbar Photography

calebtdunbar@gmail.com

www www.calebtdunbar.com

Campaign Engineers

CEO/Founder: Chris Smith

@csmithatl

csmithl911@gmail.com

Chef Batts

CEO/Founder: Keith Batts

@chefbatts

booking@chefbatts.com

Cici's Freelance Services
CEO/Founder:
   Courtney "Cici" Walker, MPA
@cicisfreelanceservices
225-288-8216
cicisfreelanceservices@gmail.com

Commit 2 Life Fitness
CEO/Founder: Joseph T. Shaw III
@commit2lifefitness
The Bitter Suite Podcast
Apple & Spotify
@thebittersuite2020
www.commit2life.com

Cjenk The Agency: Creative Concierge, LLC
CEO/Founder: Chasmin Jenkins
chasminjenkins@gmail.com

CreativeED Consulting, LLC
CEO/Founder: Dr. William J. Earvin
wjeconsulting@icloud.com

Color Wheel Therapy
CEO/Founder: Kiandra Daniels
469-251-2418
kiandra.daniels@colorwheeltherapy.com
www.colorwheeltherapy.com

Cultural Resources
CEO/Founder:
   Corey "Mr. Hanky" Dennard
@culturalresources
amrhankybeat@gmail.com

Curves & Gains

CEO/Founder: Patrice Murphy

@curvesandgaines

curvesandgains@gmail.com

www.curvesandgains.com

DD Jones Enterprise

CEO/Founder: Darcele Jones-Horton

darceleh@bellsouth.net

Da Edge 1 Productions

CEO/Founder: Garrett Edgerson

@daedge1pro

www.daedge1pro.com

DDL Entertainment

CEO/Founder: Darryl Lassister

darryldlassiter@msn.com

Daily Life Managements LLC

CEO/Founder:

Kristy Lashaun Burrell

504-390-9949

Dee Ree Hair Co

CEO/Founder: Desiree R. Dawson

desireeshanecedawson@yahoo.com

Deroune Services, LLC
CEO/Founder: Marina Zeno
337-418-0785

DS National Logistics
CEO/Founder: D. Scott
Scottie.d1911@gmail.com

Dorian Troy Studios
CEO/Founder: Dorian Davis
dorian@doriantroystudios.com

It's Demi's World Baby Dolls
CEO/Founder: Demi Scott
www.itsdemisworld.com

Dr. Ashanti Says, LLC
CEO/Founder: Dr. Ashantia Says
www.drashantisays.com
https://linktr.ee/drashantisays

Eclectikread Marketing
CEO/Founder: Christa Newkirk
@chris_ta_da
info@eclectikread.com

Elementz4 Designs, LLC
CEO/Founder: Gretta Frierson
www www.elementz4designs.com
www.linktr.ee/elementz4

Executive Reign
CEO/Founder: Canisha Cierra Turner
@Executive Reign
804-605-6875
www www.executivereign.com
www www.canishacierraturner.com

engHERneered

engHERneered
CEO/Founder: Christina Caldwell, PE
engherneered@gmail.com

February First
CEO/Founder: Cedric Livingston
Director/Writer: *February First: A Stride Towards Freedom*
www www.februaryfirstmovie.com

Enlightened Visions, Inc.
CEO/Founder: TaNisha Fordham
tanisha.fordham@gmail.com
www www.enlightenedvisions.org

Freeda's World Podcast
CEO/Founder: Ritha Pierre, Esq.
@freedas_world
accordingtorp@gmail.com

DJ General Mealz

CEO/Founder: Deitrich Armstrong

✉ dtrickarmstrong@gmail.com

Give Black App

Co-Founder/COO: Alexus Hall

⬛ @giveblackapp

⬛ @Give Black App

⬛ @giveblackapp

www www.giveblackapp.com

Happy Hour Investors

Co-Founder/Managing Partner:
  Jonathan Rivers

830 Glenwood Ave., Ste. 510-352

Atlanta, GA 30316

☎ 404-860-2288

✉ jonathan@hhinvestors.com

www www.hhinvestors.com

Harbor Institute

CEO/Founder:
  Rasheed Ali Cromwell, J.D.

⬛ @theharborinstitute

⬛ @The Harbor Institute

⬛ @harborinstitute

✉ racromwell@theharborinstitute.com

Harvey Wilder-Foundation

CEO/Founder: Jordan Harvey

www www.hawilfoundation.org

HBCU 101

CEO/Founder: Jahliel Thurman

@ @HBCU101

jahlielthurman@gmail.com

www www.hbcu101.com

The HBCU Band Experience with Christy Walker

CEO/Founder: Dr. Christy Walker

christywalker57@gmail.com

www www.christywalker.com

HBCU Buzz

(HBCU Buzz | Taper, Inc. | Root Care Health)

CEO/Founder: Luke Lawal, Jr.

@ @lukelawal

f @L & COMPANY

301-221-1719

lawal@lcompany.co

HBCU Cheer Black Excellence

@ @HBCUcheer

HBCUcheerleaders@yahoo.com

The HBCU Experience Movement, LLC

CEO/Founder: Dr. Ashley Little

@ @_ashleyalittle

f @DrAshley Little

thehbcuexperiencemovement@gmail.com

www www.thehbcuexperiencemovement.com

HBCU Girls Talk

CEO/Founder: TeeCee Camper

@HBCUgirlstalk

talkgirls@yahoo.com

HBCU Grad

CEO/Founder: Todd Finley

312-535-8511

www.hbcugraduates.com

HBCU HUB App

connects students directly to HBCUs

CEO/Founder: Dr. Darrius Brooks

@hbcuhub

www.hbcuhub.us

HBCU Legacy Fashion

CEO/Founder: Cheylaina Fultz

@HBCULegacyFashion

@HBCULegacyFashion

contact@hbculegacyfashion.com

www.hbculegacyfashion.com

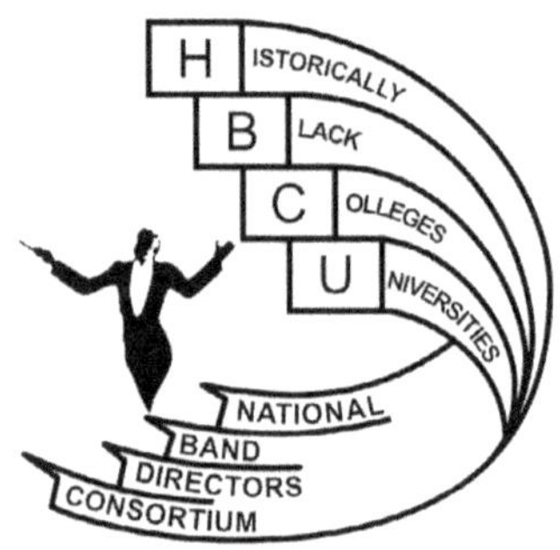

HBCU-NBDOC

www.hbcu-nbdc.org

HBCU Pride Nation

CEO/Founder: Travis Jackson

@HBCUpridenation

@HBCU Pride Nation

travispjackson@gmail.com

HBCU Pulse

CEO/Founder: Randall Barnes

@HBCUpulse

@thehbcupulse

www.hbcupulse.com

HBCU Wall Street

CEO/Founders:

Torrence Reed & Jamerus Peyton

@HBCU Wall Street

info@hbcuwallstreet.com

HBCU Recruitment Center

CEO/Founder:

Dr. Tomisha Brock-Price

3925 N. Martin Luther King Jr. Drive

Ste 209

North Las Vegas, NV 89032

hbcurecruitmentcenter@gmail.com

www.hbcurecruitmentcenter.org

H.E.R. Story Podcast

H.E.R. Story with J. Jamison

CEO/Founder: Janea Jamison

@herstory _podcast

#Herstorymovement

HBCU Times

CEO/Founders: David Staten, Ph. &

Bridget Hollis Staten, Ph.D

@HBCU_times8892

@HBCU Times

hbcutimes@gmail.com

Hidden Colours

CEO/Founder: Jahlil Witt

mr.jahlilwitt@gmail.com

Holistic Practitioners

CEO/Founder: Tianna Bynum

@Tianna Bynum

tpb33@georgetown.edu

The Hookah Bull, LLC

"An Elite Mobile Hookah Service"

Owner/Operator: Roy Ector II

301-404-9735

roy.ector@thehookahbull.com

www.thehookahbull.com

ICG Marriage & Family Therapy

CEO/Founders:

Jabari & Stephanie Walthour

@thedopesextherapist

stephanie@intimacycenterga.com

www.intimacycenterga.com

iGive

CEO/Founder: Jessica Davis

igiveglobal1@gmail.com

Johnson Capital

CEO/Founder: Marcus Johnson

@marcusdiontej

marcus@johnsoncap.com

Journee Enterprises

CEO/Founder: Fred Whit

@frederickwjr

@Fred Whit

frederickwjr@yahoo.com

J.Robins CPA, LLC

CEO/Founder: Joseph Robins

@robinscpa

@jrobinscpa

9800 Line Hwy., Ste. 261

Baton Rouge, LA 70816

225-650-7306

info@jrobinscpa.com

www.jrobinscpa.com

Kelly Collaborative Medicine

CEO/Founder: Dr. Kathyrn Kelly

10801 Lockwood Dr., Ste. 160

Silver Spring, MD 20901

301-298-1040

www.kellymedicinemd.com

K.Y. Turner Law Firm, PLLC

CEO/Founder: Khanay Turner, Esq.

khanay.turner@icloud.com

The Lab Personal and Professional Development Center, LLC

CEO/Founder: Ebony Gourrier

www.thelabppd.com

The Lady BUGS

CEO/Founder: Tatiana Tinsley Dorsey

@theladybugsoffical

@HBCU Times

ladybugs_HQ@googlegroups.com

LEMM Media Group

CEO/Founder: Cremel Nakia Burney

@cremel_the_creator

cremelburney@gmail.com

Like Minds Dine Productions

CEO/Founder: Kristin J. Meyers

✉ tokristinmeyers@gmail.com

Little Publishing, LLC

CEO/Founder: Dr. Ashley Little

⊙ @_ashleyalittle

❑ @DrAshley Little

✉ info@ashleyalittle.com

🌐 www.ashleylittleenterprises.com

Swing Into Their Dreams Foundation

Co-Founders: Pamela Parker and
   Lynn Demmons

✉ swingintotheirdreams@gmail.com

🌐 www.swingintotheirdreams.com

LK Productions

CEO/Founder: Larry King

⊙ @lk_rrproduction

❑ @Larry King

✉ lkproduction@yahoo.com

Lou's BluBooks

CEO/Founder: Louis D. Roberts

📠 202-560-7368

🌐 www.lousblubooks.com

Lynch Law, PLLC

CEO/Founder: Chance D. Lynch, Esq.

1015A Roanoke Ave., Ste. A

Roanoke Rapids, NC 27870

📠 252-535-1251

The Marching Force

700 Emancipation Dr.

Hampton, VA 23668

www www.supportthematchingforce.com

The Marching Podcast

CEO/Founder: Joseph Beard

✉ marchingpodcast@gmail.com

www www.themarchingpodcast.com

Marching Sport

CEO/Founder: Gerard Howard

✉ gerardhoward@gmail.com

McKallen Medical

CEO/Founder: Sade Stephenson,
MSN, RN, AGACNP-BC

9253 Hermosa Ave., Ste. B

Rancho Cucamonga, CA 91730

▨ 747-225-6776

✉ mckallenmedical@gmail.com

www www.mckallenmedicaltraining.com

Minority Cannabis Business Association

President: Shanita Penny

⌾ @Minority Cannabis

f @MCBA.Org

🐦 @MinCannBusAssoc

in @Minority Cannabis Business Association

▨ 202-681-2889

✉ info@minoritycannabis.org

www www.minoritycannabis.org

Mills Academy

CEO/Founder: Airneica Mills

662-822-6976

millsacademy1@gmail.com

MilRo Entertainment

CEO/Founder: Chevis Anderson

milrosplace@yahoo.com

MMarie Event Planning & Logistics

CEO/Founder: Megan Clay

meganmclay08@gmail.com

Music Greek∑, Inc.

CEO/Founder: Jeremiah Johnson

470-615-9567

musicgreeks@gmail.com

www.musicgreeks.com

NC Dance District

CEO/Founder: Dr. Kellye Worth Hall

@divadoc5

@Kellye Worth Hall

delta906@gmail.com

Never2Fly2Pray

CEO/Founder: Jeffrey Lee Sawyer

@never2fly2pray

@Jeffrey Lee

htdogwtr@yahoo.com

NXLevel Travel (NXLTRVL)

CEO: Hercules Conway

@herc3k

@Hercules Conway

COO: Newton Dennis

@nxlevel

@Newton Dennis

info@nxleveltravel.com

www.nxleveltravel.com

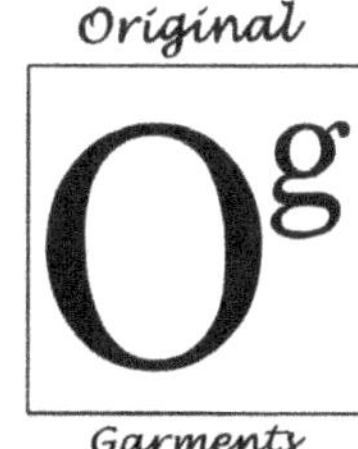

Original Garments: Clothing Brand

CEO/Founder: Dr. Darrius Brooks

@original.garments

Coming Soon (DM to purchase)

OEDM Group

CEO/Principal Owner: Justin Blake

@oedmgroup.com

contact@oedmgroup.com

www.oedmgroup.com

PacketStealer Gaming

CEO/Founder: David Matthews

packetstealer@outlook.com

The Perfect Glow

CEO/Founder: Berrie Russell

berrierussell@gmail.com

www.tpglow.com

The Phoenix Professional Network

CEO/Founder: DJavon Alston

@thephoenixnetwork757

@DJavon Alston

thephoenixnetwork757@gmail.com

Raggedi Luxury Durags
CEO/Founder: Chasmin Jenkins
✉ chasminjenkins@gmail.com

PILAR
Co-Owner: Nate Perry
📷 @barpilar
✉ nate@pilardc.com

Props Enterprises, LLC
CEO/Founders: Clarence & Keyanda
Satchell
✉ foreversatchell@gmail.com

Reach Higher
CEO/Founder: Dr. Kesha Reed
✉ info@keshareed.com

Reed Williams,
A Professional Law Corporation
CEO/Founder:
   Donald R. Williams, Jr., Esq.
9343 Tech Center Drive, Suite 165
Sacramento, CA 95826
📠 916-281-9337
🌐 www.reedwilliamslaw.com

Queen Series
CEO/Founder: Randall Barnes
✉ aqueenseries@gmail.com

Regal PhotoBooth

CEO/Founder: Kaleena Clarkson

✉ kaleenajp@gmail.com

Say Yes, LLC

CEO/Founder: Porscha Lee Taylor

⊙ @sayyesplanners

✉ info@sayyescareer.com

🌐 www.sayyesplanners.com

Reid Creative Solutions, LLC

CEO/Founder: Aja Reid

📱 919-822-2892

✉ info@reidcreativesolutions.com

🌐 www.reidcreativesolutions.com

SC DJ WORM 803

CEO/Founder: Jamie Brunson

⊙ @SCDJWORM803

f @SC DJ Worm 803

🐦 @SCDJWORM803

▣ @SC DJ Worm 803

✉ scdjworm803@gmail.com

🌐 www.scdjworm803.com

Rising Stars 3lite Cheer, Dance and Tumbling

CEO/Founders:

    Dr. Ke'Shawn Roberts and

    Ke'Shone Roberts

Central Texas

📱 504-316-9325

Seedlinks Behavior Management

CEO/Founder: Ryan L. Williams

1533 Marshall Street

Shreveport, LA 71101

📱 318-626-5597

Shani L., Relationship Enthusiast
CEO/Founder: Shani L.Farmer
@shanilrelationshipenthusiast
info@shanilfarmer.com
www.shanilfarmer.com

Special Occasion
CEO/Founder: Gary Norman II
@specialoccasionlive
www.specialoccasionlive.com

She Is Magazine
CEO/Founder: Ciara Horton
@sheisemagazine
@Ciara Horton
www.ciarasheisemagazine.com

Southern University A&M College
801 Harding Blvd.
Baton Rouge, LA 70807
225-771-4500

Shonnie Murrell
BookShonnieMurrell@gmail.com
ShonnieMurrell@gmail.com

Southern University Alumni Federation
124 Roosevelt Steptoe Dr.
Baton Rouge, LA 70807
225-771-4200
sualumni@sualumni.org

Springbreak Watches (SPGBK)

CEO/Founder: Kwame Molden

@SPGBK

@Kwame Molden

info@springbreakwatches.com

Success and Religion

CEO/Founder: Micheal Taylor

successismyreligion@gmail.com

Stamp'd Travel

CEO/Founder:

Jocelyn Hadrick Alexander

@jocehadyou

jocelyn.h.alexander@gmail.com

www.stampdtravel.com

Sugar Top Spirit & Beverage Co.

CEO/Founder: Terri White

@sugartopspirits

@sugartopspirits

tl.white412@gmail.com

www.sugartopspirits.com

Strategic Consulting, LLC

CEO/Founder:

Desiree' C. Cotton-Turner, Esq.

4917 S. Sherwood Forest Blvd.

Baton Rouge, LA 70817

225-371-3638

SwagHer

Vice President of Sales / Marketing:

Jarmel Roberson

@swaghermagazine

jroberson@swagher.net

www.swagher.net

TLW Photography
CEO/Founder: Taylor Whitehead
✉ mrknowitall91@aol.com

**The Urban Learning &
  Leadership Center, Inc.**
President/Co-Founder:
  John W. Hodge, Ed.D
✉ jhodge@ulleschools.com

Uplift Clothing Apparel
CEO/Founder: Jermaine Simpson
⊙ @upliftclothingapparel
🌐 www.upliftclothingapparel.com

Upward Path
CEO/Founder:
  Cameron Chalmers Dupree
⊙ @upwardpathtc
✉ contact@upwardpathtc.com
🌐 www.upwardpathtc.com

Urban Millennial Lifestyle
CEO/Founder: Nolita R. Pore
⊙ @themonalita
  @fitlikelita
✉ contact@themonalita.com
🌐 www.themonalita.com

The Vernon Group
Cooperative Solutions
CEO/Founder: Anthony V. Stevens
@investednu
info@vernongroupllc.com

VJR Real Estate
CEO/Founder: Victor Collins, Jr.
@vjrtherealtor
vic@thevjrgroup.com

Vision Tree, LLC
CEO/Founder: Dr. Jorim Reed
@upwardpathtc
visiontreellc@gmail.com

We Are Educated, Inc.

We Are Educated, Inc.
CEO/Founder: Ayanna Spivey
@ayannaceleste
ayanna.spivey@yahoo.com

Vision Unlimited, LLC
CEO/Founder: Kirby Denise Wilson
@Kirby_Denise_
@Kirby Denise
info@teamvisionunlimited.com
www.teamvisionunlimited.com

Yard Stubs
CEO/Founder: Cremel Burney
@YardStubs
partnerships@yardstubs.com
www.yardstubs.com

Yard Talk 101

CEO/Founder: Jahliel Thurman

@ @YardTalkl01

www www.yardtalkl01.com

Zoom Technologies, LLC

CEO/Founder: Torrence Reed

@ @torrencereed3

✉ support@zoom-technologies.co

9 798218 202750